THE INNERWORLD
OF THE OUTERWORLD
OF THE INNERWORLD

PETER HANDKE

The Innerworld of the Outerworld of the Innerworld

translated and with a Postscript by Michael Roloff

A CONTINUUM BOOK
The Seabury Press • New York

The Seabury Press
815 Second Avenue
New York, N. Y. 10017

Translation copyright © 1974 by Michael Roloff
Postscript copyright © 1974 by Michael Roloff
Editor: Michael Roloff
Designed by Paula Wiener
Printed in the United States of America

Grateful acknowledgment is made to *New American Review, Fiction, New Directions Anthology #25, University Review, Dimension, Glyph, The Literary Review* and other magazines where some of these translations first appeared.

LIBRARY OF CONGRESS CATALOGING IN PUBLICATION DATA

Handke, Peter.
    The innerworld of the outerworld of the innerworld.

    (A Continuum book)
    Poems.
    Selected from Die Innenwelt der Aussenwelt der Innenwelt.
    Bibliography: p.
    I. Roloff, Michael, tr. II. Title.
PT2668.A515213 1974   831.'9'14   73-17875
ISBN 0-8164-9194-1
ISBN 0-8164-9195-X (pbk.)

"—and in this tremulous minute the month hand of my clock rustled . . ."

". . . and since your outer and your inner world are soldered together like the two halves of a shell and enclose you, the mollusk—"

"No reply, silence throughout the inn—the whole room bathed in moon glow . . ."

JEAN PAUL

Contents

Die Innenwelt
der Außenwelt
der Innenwelt

THE INNERWORLD
OF THE OUTERWORLD
OF THE INNERWORLD

Ratschläge für einen Amoklauf

Zuerst durch ein Maisfeld rennen.
Dann in der leeren Konzerthalle durch die
                              Stuhlreihen laufen.

Dann nach dem Ende des Länderspiels sich durch den
Haupteingang zurück ins Stadion drängen.

Bist du fähig, wenn du auf die Straße trittst, nur
noch *geistesgegenwärtig* zu sein?
Bist du fähig, wenn du auf die Straße getreten bist,
dich nur noch zu *betätigen*?
Bist du fähig, wenn der Entschluß gefaßt ist, keinen
andern Entschluß mehr zu fassen?
Bist du fähig, nicht mehr Einzelheiten zu unterscheiden, sondern *Bewegungen*, nicht mehr Waagrechtes,
sondern *Aufrechtes*, nicht mehr Menschliches, sondern
Weiches?
Bist du fähig zu *allem*?

Wo versammeln sich Leute? – Leute versammeln sich,
wo sich schon Leute versammeln.
Wo versammeln sich Leute? – Vor ausgehängten
Zeitungen.
Wo versammeln sich Leute? – Vor Verkehrsampeln.
Wo noch versammeln sich Leute? – Vor Geldschaltern.

Suggestions for Running Amok

First run through a cornfield.
Then run through rows in an empty concert hall.

Then, at the end of the football game, try to get back in
the stadium through the main entrance.

When you step out on the street are you capable of having
only *presence of mind?*
When you have stepped out on the street are you capable
of being only *active?*
Once you have reached a decision are you capable of reach-
ing no *other* decision?
Are you capable of distinguishing not among particulars
but only among movements? not horizontals but only
perpendiculars, nothing human but only softness?
Are you capable of *everything?*

Where do people gather? — People gather where other
people have gathered.
Where do people gather? — In front of newspapers on dis-
play.
Where do people gather? — In front of traffic lights.
Where do people gather? — In front of bank counters.

Wo noch? – Vor Schaufenstern in Arbeit.
Wo noch? –
Vor zwei raufenden Hunden.
Vor Fleckputzmittelverkäufern.
Vor Hotelportiers, die auf die Straße treten
Wo noch? –
Unter Markisen, wenn es unversehens zu regnen
anfängt.

Es fängt zu regnen an. – Es regnet noch zu wenig.

Wo gehst du hin? – Zuerst stoße ich einen Obstkarren
um und warte, bis genug Kinder herbeilaufen, um
das Obst aufzuheben.
Und dann? – Dann verkünde ich an der Straßenecke
eine Frohe Botschaft und warte, bis genug Leute
stehengeblieben sind.
Und dann? – Dann warte ich, bis genug Leute für
jemanden ein Spalier bilden.
Und dann? – Dann stelle ich mich tot und springe
auf, wenn ich genug Leute nach einem Arzt rufen
höre.
Und dann? – Dann treibe ich eine Wette hoch, wie-
viele Leute in ein Auto passen, und warte, bis ein
Schock Leute im Auto sind.
Und dann? – Dann warte ich im Parterre eines mög-
lichst hohen Gebäudes und warte, bis der Aufzug
herunterkommt.
Und dann? – Dann werbe ich für Führungen und
warte, bis die Teilnehmer eine gewisse Mindestzahl
erreicht haben.

Where else? — In front of store windows when the display is being changed.
Where else? —
Around two dogs that fight.
Around spot-remover salesmen.
In front of hotel doormen who've stepped out on the street.
Where else?
Under awnings when it suddenly begins to rain.

It has begun to rain. — It's not raining hard enough yet.

Where are you going? — First I'll turn over the fruit cart and wait until enough children have gathered to pick up the fruit.
And then? — Then I announce the glad tidings at the street corner and wait until enough people have gathered.
And then? — Then I wait until enough people have gathered to form a lane for someone to run through.
And then? — Then I play dead and leap up when I hear enough people calling for a doctor.
And then? — Then I get people to bet on how many will fit into one car and wait until the car is crammed full.
And then? — Then I wait in the lobby, preferably of a high-rise building, and wait till the elevator reaches the lobby.
And then? — Then I advertise a tour and wait until I have assembled a minimum number of tourists.

Und dann? – Dann veröffentliche ich ein Preisausschreiben, bei dem jeder Teilnehmer einen Preis gewinnt, und warte, bis der erste Teilnehmer seinen Preis persönlich abholen möchte.

Und dann? – Zu den Telefonzellen.

Und dann? – Zur Stadtrundfahrt.

Und dann? – Bahnhofssperren.

Und dann? – Rolltreppen in Kaufhäusern.

Und dann? – Geisterbahnen.

Und dann? – Heimkehrerzüge.

Und dann? – Aussichtstürme.

Und dann? – Kurorte.

Und? – Ausfallstraßen.

Und? – Paßhöhen bei strahlendem Sonnenschein.

Und? – Beliebte Ausflugsziele.

Und? – Parkbänke in den Büropausen.

Und dann? – Fenster in Vororten bei Feierabend.

Und zuallererst? – Zuallererst beschäftige ich mich mit einem einzelnen und warte, bis sich genug Leute um den einzelnen versammelt haben.

»Die erste Schrecksekunde nützt du also dazu aus, für eine zweite Schrecksekunde zu sorgen, und die zweite Schrecksekunde, für noch eine Schrecksekunde zu sorgen, damit du, weil du ja selber von keiner Schrecksekunde betroffen bist, ihnen immer, wenn sie sich gerade von einer Schrecksekunde erholen, gerade um die weitere Schrecksekunde voraus bist, für die du gesorgt hattest, während sie sich noch von der ersten Schrecksekunde erholten, so daß schließlich die Schrecksekunden kein Ende mehr nehmen.«

And then? — Then I publicize a competition where every participant wins a prize and wait until the first participant asks to collect his prize in person.

And then? — To the telephone booths.

And then? — To the sightseeing tour.

And then? — To the department store escalators.

And then? — To the railway station at the end of the holidays.

And then? — To the observation towers.

And then? — To the resort towns.

And? — Highway exits.

And? — Mountain passes when the sun is bright and hot.

And? — Popular excursion spots.

And? — Park benches during lunch hour.

And then? — Suburban windows at supper time.

And first of all? — First of all I engage a single person and wait until enough people have gathered around that individual.

"In other words, you use the first frightful moment to make sure that there will be a second moment of fright, and the second frightful moment to make sure of a further moment of fright, so that you, since you yourself, of course, are free of fright, will always be one moment of fright ahead of them when they are just beginning to recover from their last frightful moment, for which you were responsible, while they were still recovering from the initial moment of fright, so that finally the moments of fright become legion."

Und wie?
Kurzen Prozeß machen. Nicht lang fackeln. Ausmer-
zen. Erledigen. Beiseite. Weg damit.
»Niemanden zählen lassen, nicht einmal bis drei.«

Und zuguterletzt?
Zuguterletzt lasse ich jemanden übrig, der später die
Tradition fortsetzen kann.

And how?

Make short shrift. Don't fuck around. Kill 'em off. Finish
  it up. Get it over with.
"Don't let anyone count, not even to three."

And to top it all off?
And to top it all off I spare someone to carry on the tradition.

Was ich nicht bin, nicht habe, nicht will,
nicht möchte—und was ich möchte, was ich
habe und was ich bin

(Satzbiografie)

Was ich NICHT bin:
Ich bin kein Spielverderber
Ich bin kein Kostverächter
Ich bin kein Kind von Traurigkeit.

Was ich ERSTENS, ZWEITENS und DRITTENS nicht bin:
Ich bin erstens kein Träumer, zweitens kein Einsied-
ler und drittens kein Bewohner des Elfenbeinturms.

Was ICH nicht bin:
ICH bin kein Stimmvieh.

Was ich LEIDER nicht bin:
Ich bin leider kein Held
Ich bin leider kein Millionär.

Was ich GOTTSEIDANK nicht bin:
Ich bin gottseidank kein Automat
Ich bin gottseidank keiner, mit dem man machen
kann, was man will.

What I am not, don't have, don't wish,
wouldn't like—and what I would like,
what I have and what I am

(sentence biography)

What I am NOT:
I am no spoilsport
I am no mealymouth
I am no child of sadness.

What I am not FIRST, SECOND and THIRD OF ALL:
First of all I am no dreamer, second of all I am no recluse,
    and third of all I am not an inhabitant of the ivory tower.

What *I* am not:
I am no voting bloc.

What I UNFORTUNATELY am not:
Unfortunately I am no hero
Unfortunately I am no millionaire.

What I am not THANK GOD:
Thank God I am no automat
Thank God I am not someone with whom you can do as
    you please.

Was ich SCHLIESSLICH nicht bin:
Ich bin schließlich kein Hampelmann
Ich bin schließlich kein Irrenwärter
Ich bin schließlich kein Müllabladeplatz
Ich bin schließlich kein Wohltätigkeitsverein
Ich bin schließlich kein Seelentröster
Ich bin schließlich keine Kreditanstalt
Ich bin schließlich nicht euer Fußabstreifer
Ich bin schließlich kein Auskunftsbüro.

Was ich ZWAR nicht bin, ABER AUCH nicht bin:
Ich bin zwar kein Feigling, aber auch kein
                              Lebensmüder
Ich bin zwar kein Verächter des Fortschritts, aber
                   auch kein Anbeter alles Neuen
Ich bin zwar kein Militarist, aber auch kein Verfechter
                      eines faulen Friedens
Ich bin zwar kein Anhänger von Gewalt, aber auch
                       kein Prügelknabe
Ich bin zwar kein Schwarzseher, aber auch kein blau-
                       äugiger Utopist.

Was ich WEDER NOCH bin:
Ich bin weder ein Nationalist noch ein Gleichmacher
Ich bin weder ein Anbeter der Diktatur noch ein Ver-
      teidiger einer falsch verstandenen Demokratie.

Was ich nicht HABE:
Ich habe nicht die Lust, die Nase in die Angelegen-
      heiten fremder Leute zu stecken.

What I am not AFTER ALL:
After all I am nobody's fool
After all I am no insane asylum attendant
After all I am no garbage dump
After all I am no charity organization
After all I am no soul saver
After all I am no credit union
After all I am no doormat
After all I am no information bureau.

What I ADMITTEDLY am not, BUT ALSO am not:
Admittedly I am no coward, but I am also no sadsack.
Admittedly I am no scorner of progress, but I am also no
worshipper of everything new.
Admittedly I am not a militarist, but I am also not a
proponent of a lazy peace.
Admittedly I am no supporter of violence, but I am also
no scapegoat.
Admittedly I am no pessimist, but I am also no bright-
eyed utopian.

What I am NEITHER NOR:
I am neither a nationalist nor do I believe in the abolish-
ment of all distinctions
I am neither a devotee of dictatorships nor a defender of
a misunderstood democracy.

What I don't HAVE:
I have no desire to put my nose into other people's busi-
ness.

Was ich nicht WILL:
Ich will kein Aufsehen.

Was ich nicht will, ABER:
Ich will ja nicht sagen, daß hier alles in Ordnung ist,
aber –

Was ich NICHT will, ABER AUCH nicht will:
Ich will nicht alle meine Vorzüge aufzählen, aber ich
will auch nicht auf falsche Weise bescheiden sein.

Was ich nicht MÖCHTE:
Ich möchte nicht den ersten Stein werfen.

Was ich MÖCHTE:
Ich möchte, daß wir uns vertragen.

Was ich WILL:
Ich will immer nur das Beste für euch.

Was ich GEWOLLT HABE:
Ich habe immer nur das Beste gewollt.

Was ich GEHABT HABE:
Ich habe früher ähnliche Ansichten gehabt.

Was ich HABE:
Ich habe eigene Probleme.

What I don't WANT:
I don't want a fuss.

What I don't want, BUT:
I don't want to say that everything is fine, but—

What I DON'T want, BUT ALSO don't want:
I don't want to enumerate all my good qualities, but I also
   don't want to be guilty of false modesty.

What I WOULDN'T LIKE:
I wouldn't like to cast the first stone.

What I would LIKE:
I would like for us to get along.

What I WANT:
I only want the best for you.

What I have WANTED:
I have always wanted nothing but the best.

What I USED TO HAVE:
I used to have similar opinions.

What I HAVE:
I have problems of my own.

Was ich BIN:
Ich bin dafür.

Was ich AUCH NOCH bin:
Ich bin auch noch da.

Was ich AUCH MANCHMAL bin, ABER DANN WIEDER:
Ich bin auch manchmal der Ansicht,
daß es so nicht weitergeht, aber dann wieder –

Was ich BIN:
Ich bin's!

What I AM:
I am for it.

What I STILL am.
I'm still here.

What I am ALSO SOMETIMES, BUT THEN AGAIN:
Sometimes I also feel that it can't go on like this, but then
  again—

What I AM:
It's *me*!

Die drei Lesungen des Gesetzes

1.

Jeder Staatsbürger hat das Recht –
Beifall
seine Persönlichkeit frei zu entfalten –
Beifall
insbesondere hat er das Recht auf:
Arbeit –
Beifall
Freizeit –
Beifall
Freizügigkeit –
Beifall
Bildung –
Beifall
Versammlung –
Beifall
sowie auf Unantastbarkeit der Person –
starker Beifall.

3

The Three Readings of the Law

I

Every citizen has the right —
applause
to develop his personality freely —
applause
in particular he has the right:
to work —
applause
to leisure time —
applause
to freedom of movement —
applause
to education —
applause
to assembly —
applause
and to the inviolability of his person —
loud applause

2.

Jeder Staatsbürger hat das Recht –
Beifall
im Rahmen der Gesetze seine Persönlichkeit frei zu
entfalten –
Rufe: Hört! Hört!
insbesondere hat er das Recht auf:
Arbeit entsprechend den gesellschaftlichen
Erfordernissen –
Unruhe, Beifall
auf Freizeit nach Maßgabe seiner gesellschaftlich
notwendigen Arbeitskraft –
Zischen, Beifall, amüsiertes Lachen, Unruhe
auf Freizügigkeit, ausgenommen die Fälle, in denen
eine ausreichende Lebensgrundlage nicht vorhanden
ist und der Allgemeinheit daraus besondere Lasten
entstehen würden –
schwacher Beifall, höhnisches Lachen, Scharren,
Unruhe
auf Bildung, soweit die ökonomischen Verhältnisse
sie sowohl zulassen als auch nötig machen –
starke Unruhe, Murren, unverständliche Zwischen-
rufe, Türenschlagen, höhnischer Beifall
auf Versammlung nach Maßgabe der Unterstützung
der Interessen der Mitglieder der Allgemeinheit –
Pultdeckelschlagen, Pfeifen, allgemeine Unruhe,
Lärm, vereinzelte Bravorufe, Protestklatschen, Rufe
wie: Endlich! oder: Das hat uns noch gefehlt!, Tram-
peln, Gebrüll, Platzen von Papiertüten
sowie auf Unantastbarkeit der Person –
Unruhe und höhnischer Beifall.

Every citizen has the right —
applause
to develop his personality freely within the framework of
the law —
exclamations: Hear! Hear!
in particular he has the right:
to work in accordance with the demands of society —
uneasiness, applause
to leisure time in accordance with the expenditure of
energy required by society —
hissing, applause, amused laughter, uneasiness
to freedom of movement, except in instances where the
foundation for a proper life is lacking and which would
therefore cause the general public particular hardship —
mild applause, derisive laughter, scraping of feet, uneasiness
to education insofar as economic conditions permit as well
as require it —
growing uneasiness, grumbling, incomprehensible heckling, slamming of doors, derisive laughter
to assembly insofar as this supports the interests of the general public —
pounding of table tops, whistling, general disquiet, noise, isolated shouts of bravo, rhythmic hand clapping in protest, shouts such as: Finally! or: If that doesn't take the cake! Stomping, shouting, and screaming, popping of paper bags
and to the inviolability of his person —
uneasiness and derisive applause

3.

Jeder Staatsbürger hat das Recht,
im Rahmen der Gesetze und der guten Sitten seine
Persönlichkeit frei zu entfalten,
insbesondere hat er das Recht auf Arbeit entsprechend
den wirtschaftlichen und sittlichen Grundsätzen der
Allgemeinheit –
das Recht auf Freizeit nach Maßgabe der allgemeinen
wirtschaftlichen Erfordernisse und den Möglichkeiten
eines durchschnittlich leistungsfähigen Bürgers –
das Recht auf Freizügigkeit, ausgenommen die Fälle,
in denen eine ausreichende Lebensgrundlage nicht
vorhanden ist und der Allgemeinheit dadurch besondere Lasten entstehen würden oder aber zur Abwehr
einer drohenden Gefahr für den Bestand der Allgemeinheit oder zum Schutz vor sittlicher und leistungs-
abträglicher Verwahrlosung oder zur Erhaltung eines
geordneten Ehe- Familien- und Gemeinschaftslebens –
das Recht auf Bildung, soweit sie für den wirtschaft-
lich-sittlichen Fortschritt der Allgemeinheit sowohl
zuträglich als auch erforderlich ist und soweit sie nicht
Gefahr läuft, den Bestand der Allgemeinheit in ihren
Grundlagen und Zielsetzungen zu gefährden –
das Recht auf Versammlung nach Maßgabe sowohl
der Festigung als auch des Nutzens der Allgemeinheit
und unter Berücksichtigung von Seuchengefahr,
Brandgefahr und drohenden Naturkatastrophen –
sowie das Recht auf Unantastbarkeit der Person:
Allgemeiner stürmischer, nichtendenwollender

Beifall.

3

Every citizen has the right
to develop his personality freely within the framework of
the law and standards of common decency,
in particular he has the right to work in accordance with
the economic and ethical principles of the general public —
the right to leisure time in accordance with the general
economic demands and the opportunities afforded a citizen
of average talent —
the right to freedom of movement, except in instances
where the foundation for a proper livelihood is lacking
and which would therefore cause the general public particular hardship or in defense against a threat to the very
existence of the general public or for protection against
anything that might injure the substance of the people's
moral capacity and capacity for achievement and the
preservation of an orderly marital, family and community
life —
the right to education insofar as it is beneficial to as well
as necessary for the economico-ethical progress of the
general public and except insofar as it tends to endanger
the very existence of the foundation and objectives of the
general public —
the right to assembly in accordance with the consolida-
tion of as well as the benefit to the general public and in
due consideration of the threat of epidemics, fire and
impending natural catastrophes —
as well as the right to the inviolability of his person:
General, stormy, nearly unending applause.

Die Einzahl und die Mehrzahl

Auf einer Bank im Park sitzt ein Türke mit dick
verbundenem Finger:
ich sitze auf einer Bank im Park neben einem Türken
mit dick verbundenem Finger:
wir sitzen auf einer Bank im Park, ich und ein Türke
mit dick verbundenem Finger:
Ein Türke mit dick verbundenem Finger sitzt mit mir
auf einer Bank im Park.

Wir sitzen auf einer Bank im Park und schauen hinaus auf den Teich, und ich sehe im Teich etwas
schwimmen, und der Türke schaut hinaus auf den
Teich:

Wir schauen hinaus auf den Teich, und ich sehe im
Teich einen Gegenstand schwimmen, und der Türke
schaut hinaus auf den Teich:

Wir schauen hinaus auf den Teich, und ich sehe im
Teich, von den schwimmenden Enten bewegt, ein
Grasbüschel schwimmen und auf das Ufer zu schwim-
men, und der Türke schaut hinaus auf den Teich:

Wir schauen hinaus auf den Teich, und ich sehe ein
Grasbüschel, das, von schwimmenden Enten bewegt,

4

Singular and Plural

On a bench in the park sits a Turk with a thickly bandaged finger:
I am sitting on a bench in the park next to a Turk with
 a thickly bandaged finger:
we are sitting on a bench in the park, I and a Turk with
 a thickly bandaged finger:
A Turk with a thickly bandaged finger is sitting with me
 on a bench in a park.

We are sitting on a bench in the park gazing out on the
pond, and I see something swimming in the pond, and
the Turk is gazing out on the pond:

We are gazing at the pond, and I see an object swimming
in the pond, and the Turk is gazing at the pond:

We are gazing at the pond, and I see a tuft of grass, propelled by swimming ducks, making its way to the shore,
and the Turk is gazing at the pond:

We are gazing at the pond, and I see a tuft of grass swimming shoreward, propelled by swimming ducks, and then

auf das Ufer zuschwimmt, von entgegenschwimmenden Enten bewegt, vom Ufer wegschwimmen, und
der Türke schaut hinaus auf den Teich:

Wir schauen hinaus auf den Teich, und ich sehe ein
Grasbüschel, das, von schwimmenden Enten bewegt,
daran war, ans Ufer geschwemmt zu werden, und
dann, von entgegenschwimmenden Enten bewegt,
daran war, zurück in die Mitte des Teiches geschwemmt zu werden, jetzt, von anderen, kreuzen-
den Enten bewegt, sich nur noch auf der Stelle bewegen, und der Türke schaut hinaus auf den Teich:

Wir schauen hinaus auf den Teich, und ich sehe einen
Gegenstand, den ich für ein Grasbüschel gehalten
habe, oder etwas, das ich für einen Gegenstand gehalten habe, von dem ich glaubte, daß er ein Grasbüschel sei, nachdem er sich auf der Stelle bewegt hat,
plötzlich untergehen, und auch ich höre auf, den Kopf
mit dem Gegenstand mit auf der Stelle zu bewegen:
das heißt, ich schrecke auf: oder: ich schrecke auf, das
heißt, ich höre auf, den Kopf mit dem Gegenstand
mit auf der Stelle zu bewegen, und bewege mich nicht
mehr, und der Türke schaut hinaus auf den Teich:

Wir schauen hinaus auf den Teich, und ich sehe eine
Ente auftauchen, die ein Grasbüschel im Schnabel hat,
und ich bin müde vom Schauen und zufrieden, und
der Türke schaut hinaus auf den Teich:

Wir schauen hinaus auf den Teich, und ich erinnere

I see the tuft of grass floating away from the shore, propelled by ducks swimming in the opposite direction, and the Turk is gazing at the pond:

We are gazing at the pond, and I see a tuft of grass that, propelled by swimming ducks, was about to be washed ashore and then, propelled by ducks swimming in the opposite direction, was about to be washed back into the middle of the pond and now, propelled by ducks intersecting the two groups of ducks that are swimming in opposite directions, floats suspended in place, and the Turk is gazing at the pond:

We are gazing at the pond, and I see an object I took to be a tuft of grass or something I took to be an object that I believed was a tuft of grass suddenly disappear after it had moved in place, and I stop moving my head in time with the object on one and the same spot: that is to say, I am startled or, I am startled, that is to say, I stop moving my head in time with the object on one and the same spot, and no longer move at all, and the Turk is gazing at the pond:

We are gazing at the pond, and I see a duck surfacing with a tuft of grass in its bill, and I am tired of gazing and am satisfied, and the Turk is gazing at the pond:

We are gazing at the pond, and, without seeing anything,

mich, ohne etwas zu sehen, an den Sportreporter, der vom Tod redete, und der Türke schaut hinaus auf den Teich.

Ein Türke und ich, wir sitzen im Park auf einer Bank
und schauen hinaus auf den Teich:
ich sitze im Park auf einer Bank bei einem Türken
mit dick verbundenem Finger:
ich sitze auf einer Bank im Park neben einem Türken
mit dick verbundenem Finger:
im Park sitzt plötzlich neben mir auf der Bank ein
Türke mit einem dick verbundenen Finger, den er
von den anderen wegstreckt:
im Park auf einer Bank sitzt ein Türke mit neun
heilen Fingern, die er an sich drückt:
auf einer Bank im Park sitzt ein Türke mit dick verbundenem Finger und schaut hinaus auf den Teich.

I remember the sports writer who talked about death, and the Turk is gazing at the pond:

A Turk and I, we are sitting in the park on a bench and
    are gazing at the pond:
I am sitting in the park on a bench next to a Turk with a
    thickly bandaged finger:
I am sitting on a bench in the park next to a Turk with a
    thickly bandaged finger:
next to me on the bench in the park there suddenly sits a
    Turk with a thickly bandaged finger which he is ex-
    tending away from his other fingers:
in the park on a bench sits a Turk with nine unimpaired
    fingers which he presses to the palms of his hands:
on a bench in the park sits a Turk with a thickly bandaged
    finger and gazes at the pond.

5

Die Besitzverhältnisse

Mit dem Wort ICH fangen schon die Schwierigkeiten an.

Mehrere Herren
haben schon vor geraumer Zeit einige Flaschen Sekt
bestellt;
ein Reisender
kehrt aus dem Speisewagen zum Abteil zurück;
die Hundertmeterläufer
versammeln sich nach dem Fehlstart wieder vor
den Startlöchern;
und der Kriegsversehrte
locht in der Bahnhofssperre die Fahrkarten:

Wo bleibt UNSER Sekt? rufen die Herren dem Kellner
zu, der ohne *ihren* Sekt an den Herren vorbeieilt;
das ist MEIN Platz! ruft der Reisende dem anderen
Reisenden zu, der sich auf *seinem* Platz breitgemacht
hat;
verzieh dich aus MEINEM Startloch! ruft der Hundertmeterläufer dem andern Hundertmeterläufer zu, der
mit der Schuhspitze das Startloch des ersten Hundert-
meterläufers erweitert;
ich lasse mir MEINEN Stolz nicht rauben! ruft der
Kriegsversehrte dem Betrunkenen zu, der ihm, indem

5

Conditions of Ownership

With the word *I* the difficulties set in.

Several gentlemen
ordered a bottle of champagne some time ago;
a traveler
returns from the dining car to his compartment;
the hundred-yard sprinters
are reassembling at the starting holes after a false start;
and the disabled veteran
is punching tickets at the railroad gate:

What happened to OUR champagne? the gentlemen call
to the waiter as he rushes past without *their* champagne;
that's MY seat! says the traveler to the other traveler who
has made himself comfortable in *his* seat;
remove yourself from MY starting hole! says the sprinter
to the other sprinter who is digging with the tip of his
shoe in *his* starting hole;
I won't let anyone rob me of MY pride! shouts the disabled

er sich über die Arbeit in der Bahnhofssperre lustig
macht, *seinen* Stolz rauben will:

MEIN:
der Machtspruch des Herrschers über SEINE Untertanen
die Dankadresse der Untertanen an IHREN Herrscher
die Anklagemöglichkeit des Beraubten
die Verteidigungsmöglichkeit des Räubers
. die Hilfsmöglichkeit des seiner selbst nicht mehr
Bewußten
die Bestätigungsmöglichkeit des Selbstbewußten:

Das war MEINE Stunde! schreibt der Staatsmann in
seinen Erinnerungen;
das ist MEIN Bild! ruft verwundert der zum ersten
Mal Abgebildete;
MEIN Patient hat flüssige Nahrung zu sich nehmen
können! ist die Auskunft des Arztes, als für den
Kranken wieder Hoffnung besteht;
das ist MEIN Berg! notiert der Erstbesteiger ins Tage-
buch, nachdem er den Wimpel seines Landes in den
Schnee auf dem Gipfel gesteckt hat;
wo ist MEIN Japaner? erkundigt sich der Gastgeber
einer Abendgesellschaft, zu der auch ein Japaner
gehört:

MEIN:
der Anspruch der Größeren auf das Kleinere,
Vertraute
aber auch die Beschwörung der Kleineren
für das nicht Geheure, nicht Vertraute

veteran to the drunk who, ridiculing his work at the railroad gate, wants to rob him of *his* pride:

MINE:
the ruler's decree to HIS subjects
the subjects' expression of gratitude toward THEIR ruler
the robbery victim's opportunity to accuse
the robber's opportunity to defend himself
The opportunity of someone unconscious of himself to
    help himself
The opportunity of the self-assured to assert himself:

That was MY hour! the statesman writes in his memoirs;
that is MY picture! exclaims the man who has been por-
trayed for the first time;
MY patient was able to absorb liquid nourishment! is the
doctor's statement when there is new hope for the patient;
that is MY mountain! the mountain climber who has made
the first ascent notes down in his diary after he has
planted his country's flag in the snow on the mountain
top;
where is MY Japanese? the host inquires at a party to which
a Japanese guest has been invited;

MY:
the potentate's claim on what is impotent, familiar
but also the impotent man's beseeching
of what is ominous, unfamiliar

damit das Nichtgeheure vertraut wird:

MEINE Welt und
MEINE Angelegenheiten und
MEIN Inneres und
MEINE Erinnerung:

Als eine Möglichkeit sich zu behaupten
aber auch als eine Möglichkeit sich zu fügen:

MEIN Wellensittich (die Frau nach dem Unglück das
                            ihr sonst alles genommen hat)
MEIN Land (der Grundbesitzer am Morgen)
MEIN Schuhputzer (der Schriftsteller Willy Haas
                            an Hugo v. Hofmannsthal)
MEIN Staat (der Grundbesitzer am Abend):

MEIN
gebraucht der Kommissar für den Mord, den er
                                        aufklärt
aber nicht für den Mord an sich selber;
gebraucht der Häftling für seine Zelle
aber nicht für das ganze Gefängnis;
gebraucht der Fluggast für seinen Fensterplatz
aber nicht wenn die Maschine schon abstürzt;
gebraucht der Arbeiter für sein Produkt
aber nicht vor dem Dienstherrn;
gebraucht der Untersuchte für sein Röntgenbild
aber nur wenn es zeigt daß er gesund ist;
MEIN
sagt das Kind für sein Spielzeug
aber nicht für sich selber:

so that what is ominous may become familiar:

MY world and
MY affairs and
MY insides and
MY memories:

As an opportunity to assert oneself
but also as an opportunity for compromise:

MY canary (the woman, after the accident has deprived
  her of everything else)
MY land (the estate owner at sunrise)
MY shoeshine boy (the writer Willy Haas to Hugo v.
  Hoffmannsthal)
MY state (the estate owner at sunset):

MY
the police commissioner applies to the murder which he
  solves
but not to the murder committed on himself;
the prisoner applies to his cell
but not to the prison;
the airline passenger applies to his window seat
but not to the plane that crashes;
the worker applies to his product
but not in front of his employer;
the patient applies to his X-ray picture
but only if it shows that he is well;
the child says of its toy
but not of itself:

35

MEINE Lebensmüden! sagt die Pflegerin des
                                    Lebensmüdenheims;
MEINE Küche! sagt die verheiratete Frau;
MEIN Außenminister! sagt der Regierungschef;
MEIN Gott! sagt der Erschreckte:

und wir sprechen und hören von
UNSERER Wirklichkeit
sowie von
MEINEM Lieblingsgericht
und auch von
UNSEREM Goldvorrat
und auch von
MEINEM Hochzeitsbild
und nicht zuletzt von
UNSEREN damals schuldlos Verurteilten:

aber niemand spricht und hört von
UNSERER berittenen Polizei oder
UNSEREN Hungerbäuchen und
UNSEREN Jüngsten Tagen oder
UNSEREN Schüssen in einen mit Wasser gefüllten
                                    Mund und
UNSEREN Kothaufen oder
UNSEREN Sägespänen für Geköpfte und
UNSEREN betrunkenen Kutschern unter den Kirchen-
                                    treppen oder
UNSEREN Selbstmorddunkelziffern —

zu schweigen
von den Fällen

MY invalids! says the nurse who works in the nursing
    home;
MY kitchen! says the married woman;
MY foreign minister! says the head of government;
MY God! says someone who's startled:

and we speak and hear of
OUR reality
as well as of
MY favorite dish
and also of
OUR gold reserves
and also of
MY marriage portrait
and last but not least of
OUR falsely condemned:

but no one speaks or hears of
OUR mounted police or
OUR hungry stomachs and
OUR Judgment Days or
OUR shots into a mouth filled with water and
OUR pile of shit or
OUR sawdust for the beheaded and
OUR drunken coachmen under the church stairways or
OUR obscure suicide statistics —

not to speak
of the cases

bei denen es sich nicht *lohnt*
von MEIN und UNSER zu sprechen:
zum Beispiel von
MEINEM wurmstichigen Apfel
zum Beispiel von
UNSERER zerbrochenen Glühbirne
zum Beispiel von
MEINEM naßgewordenen Streichholz –

zu schweigen auch
von dem Fall
des Vaters
der vor der Leiche seines von den Zwillingsreifen eines
Lastwagens verstümmelten Kindes sagt:
das ist NICHT meine Tochter
das ist NICHT meine Tochter –

zu schweigen auch
von dem Fall
des Verrückten
der unentwegt ausruft:
das ist NICHT meine Stimme
das ist NICHT meine Stimme –

und auch
von dem Fall
des steckbrieflich Gesuchten
der vor dem Bild auf dem Steckbrief beteuert:
das bin nicht ICH
das bin nicht ICH

zu schweigen

where it is hardly worthwhile
to speak of MY and OUR:
for example of
MY wormeaten apple
for example of
OUR broken light bulb
for example of
MY match that got wet —

nor to speak
of the case
of the father
who, standing by the corpse of the child mangled by the
  twin tires of a truck, says:
that is NOT my daughter
that is NOT my daughter —

nor to speak
of the case
of the madman
who shouts incessantly:
that is NOT my voice
that is NOT my voice —

nor of the case
of the wanted man
who insists in front of the wanted poster:
that's not ME
that's not ME

not to speak

Die verkehrte Welt

Eingeschlafen wache ich auf:
Ich schaue nicht auf die Gegenstände, und die Gegen-
stände schauen mich an;
Ich bewege mich nicht, und der Boden unter meinen
Füßen bewegt mich;
Ich sehe mich nicht im Spiegel, und ich im Spiegel
sehe mich an;
Ich spreche nicht Wörter, und Wörter sprechen mich
aus;
Ich gehe zum Fenster und werde geöffnet.

Aufgestanden liege ich da:
Ich schlage die Augen nicht auf, sondern die Augen
schlagen mich auf;
Ich horche nicht auf die Geräusche, sondern die Ge-
räusche horchen auf mich;
Ich schlucke das Wasser nicht, sondern das Wasser
schluckt mich;
Ich greife nicht nach den Gegenständen, sondern die
Gegenstände greifen mich an;
Ich entledige mich nicht der Kleider, sondern die
Kleider entledigen sich meiner;
Ich rede mir nicht Wörter ein, sondern Wörter reden
mich mir aus;
Ich gehe zur Tür, und die Klinke drückt mich nieder.

6

The Inverted World

I wake up asleep:
I don't look at the objects, and the objects look at me;
I don't move, and the ground under my feet moves me;
I don't see myself in the mirror, and I in the mirror see
   myself;
I don't pronounce words, and words pronounce me;
I go to the window and I am opened.

I lie there upright:
I don't open my eyes, but my eyes open me;
I don't listen to sounds, but sounds listen to me;
I don't swallow water, but water swallows me;
I don't reach for objects, but objects reach for me;
I don't take off my clothes, but my clothes take me off;
I don't talk words into myself, but words talk me out of
   myself;
I go to the door, and the handle presses me down.

Die Rollbalken werden hinaufgelassen, und es wird
Nacht, und um nach Luft zu schnappen, tauche ich
unters Wasser:

Ich trete auf den Steinboden und sinke knöcheltief
ein;
Ich sitze auf dem Bock einer Kutsche und setze einen
Fuß vor den andern;
Ich sehe eine Frau mit einem Sonnenschirm, und der
Nachtschweiß bricht mir aus;
Ich strecke den Arm in die Luft, und er fängt Feuer;
Ich greife nach einem Apfel und werde gebissen;
Ich gehe mit bloßen Füßen und spüre einen Stein im
Schuh;
Ich reiße das Pflaster von der Wunde, und die Wunde
ist im Pflaster;
Ich kaufe eine Zeitung und werde überflogen;
Ich erschrecke jemanden zu Tode und kann nicht
mehr reden;
Ich stecke mir Watte in die Ohren und schreie;
Ich höre die Sirenen heulen, und der Fronleichnams-
zug führt an mir vorbei;
Ich spanne den Regenschirm auf, und der Boden
brennt mir unter den Füßen;
Ich laufe ins Freie und werde verhaftet.

Über den Parkettboden stolpere ich,
mit weit offenem Mund führe ich Konversation,
mit den Handballen kratze ich,
mit der Trillerpfeife lache ich,
aus den Haarspitzen blute ich,

The shutters are rolled up and it becomes
Night, and to catch a breath of air I dive under water:

I step on the stone floor and sink in ankle-deep;
I sit on the box of the coach and put one foot before the
    other;
I see a woman with a parasol and break out in a cold sweat;
I raise my arm in the air and it catches fire;
I reach for an apple and I am bitten;
I walk on bare feet and feel a stone in my shoe;
I tear the bandaid from the wound and the cut is in the
    bandaid;
I buy a newspaper and I am scanned;
I frighten someone to death and am left aghast;
I stuff cotton in my ears and scream;
I hear sirens wailing and the Corpus Christi procession
    passes by;
I open the umbrella and the ground singes my feet;
I run into the open and am arrested.

It is over the floor that I trip,
and with a wide open mouth that I make conversations,
and with the palm of my hand that I scratch myself,
and with the police whistle that I laugh,
and out of the ends of my hair that I bleed,

am Aufschlagen der Zeitung ersticke ich,
wohlriechende Speisen erbreche ich,
von der Zukunft erzähle ich,
zu Sachen rede ich,
mich durchschaue ich,
Tote töte ich.

Und die Spatzen sehe ich auf die Kanonen schießen;
und den Verzweifelten sehe ich glücklich sein;
und den Säugling sehe ich Wünsche haben;
und den Milchmann sehe ich am Abend:

: und der Briefträger? fragt nach Post;
und der Prediger? wird aufgerüttelt;
und das Erschießungskommando? stellt sich an die
           Wand;
und der Clown? wirft eine Granate unter die
           Zuschauer;
und der Mord? geschieht erst beim Lokalaugenschein.

Und der Leichenbestatter feuert seine Fußballmann-
           schaft an;
Und das Staatsoberhaupt verübt ein Attentat auf den
           Bäckerlehrling;
Und der Feldherr wird nach einer Gasse benannt;
Und die Natur wird getreu nach einem Bild gemalt;
Und der Papst wird stehend ausgezählt –

und hör! Die Uhr geht außerhalb ihrer selbst!
Und schau! Die herabbrennenden Kerzen werden
           größer!

and on opening the newspaper that I choke,
and caviar that I regurgitate,
and I tell about the future,
and I talk to things,
and it is through *myself* that I see,
and corpses that I kill.

And I see sparrows firing at cannons;
and I see the catatonic in ecstasy;
and I see the newborn baby actually having wishes;
and I see the milkman at night:

:and the letter carrier? asks for the mail;
and the preacher? rolls on the ground;
and the firing squad? lines up against the wall;
and the clown? flings a grenade among the spectators;
and the murder? does not occur until the eyewitnesses
   appear.

And the mortician cheers his soccer team;
And the head of state attempts to assassinate the baker's
   apprentice;
And the field marshall is named after a side street;
And nature is faithfully reproduced after a painting;
And the Pope is counted out standing up—

and listen! The watch ticks outside itself!
And look! The guttering candles are growing!

Und hör! Der Schrei wird geflüstert!
Und schau! Der Wind versteinert das Gras!
Und hör! Das Volkslied wird gebrüllt!
Und schau! Der erhobene Arm weist nach unten!
Und hör! Das Fragezeichen wird befohlen!
Und schau! Der Verhungerte ist fett!
Und riech! Der Schnee fault!

Und es neigt sich der Morgen,
und auf einem Bein steht der Tisch,
und im Schneidersitz sitzt der Flüchtling,
und im obersten Stockwerk befindet sich die Halte-
        stelle der Straßenbahn:

   ————————————

Horch! Es ist totenstill! – Es ist Hauptgeschäftszeit!

   ————————————

Aufgewacht bin ich eingeschlafen
und flüchte mich aus dem unerträglichen Traum in die
        sanfte Wirklichkeit
und summe fröhlich Zeter und Mordio –
horch, wie mir das Wasser im Mund zusammenrinnt:
        ich sehe eine Leiche!

And listen! The scream is whispered!
And look! The wind petrifies the grass!
And listen! The folk song is bellowed!
And look! The raised arm points down!
And listen! The question mark is commanded!
And look! The starved man is fat!
And smell! The snow is rotting!

And it is morningfall,
and the table stands on one leg,
and the escapee assumes the lotus position,
and the trolley stops on the forty-ninth floor:

——————————

Listen! It is deathly quiet!—It is rush hour.

——————————

I fell asleep awake
and fled the unbearable dream for gentle reality
and am humming hue and cry to myself, merrily as they
    say—
listen to my mouth watering: I see a corpse!

Steigerungen

Es ist nicht von vornherein ganz auszuschließen,
daß der Parkwächter gleich unglücklich sein kann
wie der Schlagersänger
der Volksschullehrer
und der Machthaber:
aber es ist die Regel,
daß der Schlagersänger unglücklicher ist als der Parkwächter und der Volksschullehrer unglücklicher als
                              der Schlagersänger –
und die Wahrscheinlichkeit,
daß der Machthaber der unglückseligste von allen ist,
grenzt in der Regel schon an Gewißheit.

Ebenso
ist es nicht ganz von der Hand zu weisen,
daß das Sonntagshemd des Landarbeiters gleich kurze
                              Ärmel haben kann
wie das Alltagshemd des Sheriffs aus Mississippi
das Freizeithemd des rhodesischen Bürgers
und das Feierabendhemd des Lynchmörders:
aber es scheint sicher,
daß das Alltagshemd des Sheriffs kürzere Ärmel hat
            als das Sonntagshemd des Landarbeiters
und daß das Freizeithemd des rhodesischen Bürgers
kürzere Ärmel hat als das Alltagshemd des Sheriffs –

Augmentations

It is not entirely inconceivable at first
that the night watchman can be just as unhappy
as the pop singer
the public school teacher
and the potentate:
but as a rule
the pop singer is unhappier than the night watchman and
the public school teacher is unhappier than the pop
singer —
and the likelihood
that the potentate is the most miserable of them all
borders as a rule on absolute certainty.

By the same token
the possibility cannot be dismissed out of hand
that the sleeves of the migrant worker's Sunday shirt are
just as short
as the sleeves of the work shirt of the sheriff from Mississippi
the sport shirt of the Rhodesian citizen
and the dress shirt of the mobster:
but it seems certain
that the sheriff's work shirt will have shorter sleeves than
the migrant worker's Sunday shirt
and that the Rhodesian citizen's sport shirt will have
shorter sleeves than the work shirt of the sheriff —

und es ist unbestritten,
daß das Feierabendhemd des Lynchmörders die
kürzesten Ärmel von allen hat.

Und ebenso
kann die Farbe des Briefkastens am Postamt gleich
gelb sein
wie die Farbe des Briefkastens an der
Milchsammelstelle
die Farbe des Briefkastens an der Landstraße am
Sonntagnachmittag
und die Farbe des Briefkastens im Hitchcockfilm:
aber
in neunhundertneunundneunzig von tausend Fällen
ist der Briefkasten an der Milchsammelstelle gelber
als der Briefkasten am Postamt
und der Briefkasten an der Landstraße am Sonntagnachmittag gelber als der Briefkasten an der Milchsammelstelle –
und in tausend von tausend Fällen hat der Briefkasten im Hitchcockfilm das schreiendste Gelb von
allen.

Und schließlich
können die Fremdenführer ohne Frage einen guten
Willen haben
aber
die Fußballordner haben ohne Frage einen besseren
Willen als die Fremdenführer
und die Tarifpartner haben den besseren Willen als
die Fremdenführer

and there is no disputing the fact
that the mobster's dress shirt has the shortest sleeves of
them all.

And similarly
the color of the mailbox at the post office can be just as
yellow
as the color of the mailbox at the milk-collecting station
the color of the mailbox on the country road on a Sunday
afternoon
and the color of the mailbox in a Hitchcock film:
but
in nine hundred and ninety-nine out of a thousand cases
the mailbox at the milk-collecting station will be yellower
than the mailbox at the post office
and the mailbox on the country road on a Sunday afternoon will be yellower than the mailbox at the milk-collecting station —
and in a thousand out of a thousand cases the mailbox in
the Hitchcock film will be the most excruciating yellow
of them all.

And finally
tourist guides unquestionably are able to be of good will

but
the ushers at football games are unquestionably of better
will than the tourist guides
and the tariff partners of better will than the tourist guides

und die reuigen Sünder haben trotz allem einen
besseren Willen als die Tarifpartner
und jeder Tote hatte zumindest den besseren Willen
als jeder reuige Sünder –
aber der die Macht zu wollen hat, hat fraglos den
besten Willen von allen.

and despite everything the will of repentant sinners is
better than that of tariff partners
and every dead man has at least a better will than every
repentant sinner —
but whoever has the power to will has without question
the best will of them all.

Abstraktion von dem Ball, der in den Fluss gefallen ist

Als Kinder saßen wir am Sonntagnachmittag oft am Ufer des Flusses und schauten dort, an der Feldmitte, dem Fußballspiel zu. Sooft der Ball an unserer Stelle ins Wasser fiel, liefen wir den Fluß entlang, um mit langen Stangen den Ball aus dem Wasser zu fischen. Wir konnten uns dabei Zeit lassen, weil jedesmal, wenn der Ball ins Wasser fiel, vom Spielfeldrand sogleich ein Reserveball aufs Spielfeld geworfen wurde. Wir liefen so schnell wie der Ball vom Fluß getragen wurde, bis wir ihn jedesmal, kurz vor der Wehrmauer, herausfischten. Der Fluß war in der Regel so ruhig, daß wir meistens neben dem Ball hergehen konnten. Als aber einmal Hochwasser war, mußten wir laufen.

Am Rand eines Fußballplatzes, der an einem Fluß liegt, pflegt sich eine Anzahl von Kindern einen Spaß daraus zu machen, jedesmal, wenn der Ball im Verlauf des Spiels ins Wasser fällt, von der Höhe der Spielfeldmitte aus gerade bis zum Spielfeldende neben dem Ball herzulaufen, um ihn dort erst aus dem Wasser zu holen. Als der Fluß einmal Hochwasser führt, müssen die Kinder sehr schnell laufen.

Abstraction of the Ball that
Fell in the River

As children we often sat at the edge of the river Sunday afternoons watching the soccer game from where we sat at the midfield line. Whenever the ball fell in the water near where we were sitting we ran alongside the river and with long poles fished the ball out of the water. We could take our time doing this since each time the ball fell in the water another ball that was kept in reserve was put into play from the sideline. We ran as fast as the ball was carried along by the river until we fished it out always just before it reached the wall of the weir. As a rule, the river flowed slowly enough so all we had to do was walk alongside the ball. But once when the river was swollen we had to run.

At the edge of a soccer field that is situated by a river, a number of children are in the habit of amusing themselves by running alongside the ball whenever it falls into the river during the course of play; that is, they run alongside the ball from the midfield line to the end of the field and fish it out of the water only there. Once the river is swollen, and the children have to run very quickly.

Kinder gehen jedesmal neben dem Ball her, wenn dieser auf der Höhe der Mittellinie eines Fußballfeldes in einen Fluß fällt. Erst am Ende des Fußballfeldes fischen sie den Ball aus dem Wasser. Bei Hochwasser laufen die Kinder sehr schnell.

Personen gehen von der Mittellinie eines Fußballfelds bis zum Ende des Fußballfelds neben einem Gegenstand her, der im Fluß am Rand des Spielfelds treibt. Als sie gerade am Ende des Fußballfelds angelangt sind, pfeift der Schiedsrichter zur Halbzeit. Bei Hochwasser, als die Personen laufen müssen, machen sie auf der Höhe des Gegenstands am Spielfeldende kurz vor dem Halbzeitpfiff Halt.

Jemand geht am Rand eines Fußballplatzes neben einem Gegenstand her, der in den Fluß gefallen ist. Er setzt sich 30 Sekunden vor der letzten Minute der Halbzeit von der Spielfeldmitte aus in Bewegung. Als er, genau auf der Höhe des Gegenstands, das Spielfeldende erreicht hat, pfeift der Schiedsrichter zur Halbzeit. Bei Hochwasser erreicht er das Spielfeldende, nachdem er sich zugleich mit dem Gegenstand 10 Sekunden vor dem Halbzeitpfiff des Schiedsrichters in Bewegung gesetzt hat, zugleich mit dem Gegenstand 1 Sekunde vor dem Abpfiff.

Jemand benötigt, um die Hälfte der Länge eines Spielfelds (Spielfeldlänge = 90 Meter) zurückzulegen, 1 Minute und 30 Sekunden. Als er laufen muß, benötigt er für dieselbe Strecke nur 9 Sekunden.

Children walk alongside the ball each time it falls in the river at midfield. They fish the ball out of the water only at the end of the field. When the river is swollen the children run very quickly.

Persons walk from the midfield line of a soccer field to the end of the field alongside an object that is drifting in the river at the edge of the field. At the moment when they reach the end of the field the referee whistles half-time. When the river is swollen and the persons have to run they come to a stop alongside the object at the end of the field shortly before the half-time whistle blows.

Someone is walking along the edge of a soccer field next to an object that has fallen in the river. He gets under way 30 seconds before the last minute of the first half of the game. At the very moment he has reached the end of the field and stands next to the object the referee blows the half-time whistle. When the river is swollen he reaches the end of the field together with the object precisely one second before the whistle blows and after he has gotten under way simultaneously with the object 10 seconds before the referee blows his whistle.

In order to traverse half the length of a playing field (playing field length = 90 meters) someone requires 1 minute, 30 seconds. When he has to run he requires for the same distance only 9 seconds.

Jemand benötigt für 45 Meter 90 Sekunden. Laufend benötigt er 9 Sekunden.

---

90 sec———45 m
1 sec———Geschwindigkeit x m

9 sec———45 m
1 sec———Geschwindigkeit y m

$$90 \, x = 45$$
$$9 \, y = 45$$
$$x = \frac{45}{90}$$
$$y = \frac{45}{9}$$
$$x = \frac{1}{2}$$
$$y = 5$$

Als Kinder gingen wir am Sonntagnachmittag mit einer Geschwindigkeit von einem halben Meter in der Sekunde neben dem Ball her, wenn dieser vom Spielfeld in den Fluß geschossen wurde. Aber als einmal Hochwasser war, mußten wir mit einer Geschwindigkeit von fünf Metern in der Sekunde neben dem Ball herlaufen, um ihn herauszufischen, bevor er über die Wehrmauer fiel.

It takes someone 90 seconds to traverse 45 meters. Running it takes him 9 seconds.

90 sec————45 m
  1 sec————speed x m

  9 sec————45 m
  1 sec————speed y m

$90 x = 45$
$9 y = 45$
$x = \dfrac{45}{90}$
$y = \dfrac{45}{9}$
$x = \dfrac{1}{2}$
$y = 5$

As children we walked on Sunday afternoons at a speed of one half meter per second alongside the soccer ball when it was kicked from the playing field into the river. But when the river was swollen we had to run alongside the ball at a speed of five meters per second to fish the ball out of the water before it would be washed over the wall of the weir.

Der Rand der Wörter 2

Wir sitzen am Rand des Feldwegs und reden.
Die größte Not ist lange vorbei, denn am Gletscher-
rand lagern die Leichen ab.
Wer steht am Rand des Feldes, am Rand des High-
way? – Cary Grant!
Am Grubenrand liegt, vom Spaten gespalten, ein
Engerling.
Der Rand des Schmutzflecks trocknet schon.
Es wird bitter kalt, und dem Captain Scott fängt die
Wunde vom Rand her zu eitern an.
Am Rand der Erschöpfung reden wir alle in Haupt-
sätzen.
Von den schmutzigen Taschen des Toten haben die
Fingernägel des Plünderers einen Rand.
Wir sitzen am Rand des Feldwegs, am Rand des
Feldes, und reden, und reden.
Wo der Rand der Wörter sein sollte, fängt trockenes
Laub an den Rändern zu brennen an, und die Wörter
krümmen sich unendlich langsam in sich selber:
»Diese Trauerränder!«
Dieser Rand der Trauer.

The Edge of Words 2

We sit at the edge of the dirt road and talk.

The direst need has long since passed, for the bodies are being piled up at the edge of the glacier.

Who's that standing at the edge of the field, at the edge of the highway? — Cary Grant!

At the edge of the ditch, split by the spade, lies a cockchafer grub.

It is turning bitter cold and Captain Scott's wound is beginning to fester at the edges.

At the edge of exhaustion we all speak in principal sentences.

The scavenger's fingernails are edged in black from the dead man's dirty pockets.

We're sitting at the edge of the dirt road, at the edge of the dirt road, and talk, and talk.

Where the edge of the words ought to be, dry leaves are catching fire at the edges and the words are curling into themselves infinitely slowly:

"These edges of sorrow!"

This edge of sorrow.

Die Innenwelt der Aussenwelt der Innenwelt

»Wir«:

Erst als der Erschossene abtransportiert wird
erkennen wir
an den großen runden Nagelköpfen
an der Schuhsohle des Erschossenen
daß dieser unschuldig war

Wir sind in Nashville in Tennessee:
aber als wir das Hotelzimmer betreten
und die Nummer des PLAYBOY
mit dem zum Teil sichtbaren schimmernden
                              Naseninnern
der Ursula Andress
angeschaut haben
greift
– statt der Ratlosigkeit darüber
daß wir in Nashville sind –
das Naseninnere der Ursula Andress um sich

Wir gehen nach Prag:
dort ist es gegen neun Uhr am Abend
wir lesen von der Zeit der Stille auf den Straßen
aber als wir um neun Uhr auf die Straße treten
ist es höchste Zeit

The Innerworld of the
Outerworld of the Innerworld

"WE":

Only when they carry out the one who's been shot
do we recognize
by the big round nail heads
on the soles of the boots of the one who's been shot
that he was innocent

We are in Nashville, Tennessee:
but when we enter the hotel room
and have looked at the issue of PLAYBOY
with the partially visible, glinting inside
of Ursula Andress's nose
what begins to seize us
—in lieu of perplexity over the fact
that we are in Nashville—
is the inside of Ursula Andress's nose

We go to Prague:
there it is around nine in the evening
we read about the time of quiet in the streets
but when we step on the street at nine
it is high time

für den letzten Versuch
ohne Gesellschaft zu bleiben

Wir befinden uns in einem Warenhaus:
wir wollen die Rolltreppe benutzen
um in die Spielwarenabteilung zu gelangen
wo wir Bauklötze kaufen wollen
aber da die Rolltreppe im Augenblick steht
verwandelt sich die stehende Rolltreppe
auf der wir nach oben gehen
in unseren angehaltenen Atem
und der angehaltene Atem
den wir jetzt ausstoßen
weil sich die Rolltreppe plötzlich wieder bewegt
stürzt zusammen zu einem Haufen von Bauklötzen –

Wir gehen in uns:
dort ist es
wenn wir wütend sind
spät am Nachmittag wie in einem Tatsachenbericht
                              über ein Attentat:
wenn wir müde werden
lassen uns dort die lückenlos hängenden Schlüssel an
                    einem Hotel-Schlüsselbrett
die Augen zufallen:
mit dem Mond geht dort
die Besänftigung auf:
das Erstaunen verwandelt sich in ein weißes Tuch
das nach Feierabend die Süßigkeiten in einer
                              Konditorei
bedeckt:
und mit der Scham

for a last-ditch effort
to stay alone

We find ourselves in a department store:
we want to use the escalator
to get to the toy department
where we want to purchase building blocks
but since the escalator has temporarily stopped
the immobile escalator
on which we are walking up
transforms itself into our breath
which we are holding
and the held breath
which we now exhale
because the escalator is suddenly moving again
implodes into a pile of building blocks—

We go inside ourselves:
there
when we are furious
it is late afternoon as in a factual report about an assassina-
    tion:
when we become tired
all the keys dangling on their appointed hooks on the
    hotel key rack make
our eyelids drop:
at the same time as the moon
appeasement rises there:
astonishment transforms itself into a white sheet
covering the sweets in a candy store after closing time:
and together with the feeling of shame

überfällt uns dort der Akrobat im Zirkus
der nach seiner mißglückten Nummer mit dem
                                    strahlenden
Lächeln die Arme ausbreitet –

Als wir einmal sorglos sind
sehen wir einen Waldläufer in einem blauen
                                    Trainingsanzug
an uns vorbeilaufen
aber dann sehen wir
daß der Waldläufer eine Straße hinunterläuft:
weil wir nicht mehr sorglos sind;
und sehen schließlich
daß der Waldläufer nicht in einem Trainingsanzug
                                    die Straße
hinabläuft
sondern in einem langen Mantel
der ihn beim Laufen behindert:
weil wir unruhig sind;
und sehen dann
während wir uns im Zug aus den Fenstern lehnen
wie der Waldläufer im blauen Trainingsanzug uns
                                    zuwinkt:
zum Zeichen
daß wir wieder sorglos sind –

Die Beklemmung verwandelt sich in eine grüne
                                    Ampel
auf die wir zugehen
während sie noch grün ist
und die gelbe Ampel

we are overcome
   by the acrobat in
the circus who, after his number has failed, with a beam-
   ing smile
spreads his arms wide—

Once when we are without a care in the world
we see a cross-country runner in a blue sweat suit
running past us
but then we see
that the cross-country runner is running down a street:
because we are no longer without a care in the world;
and finally we see
that the cross-country runner is not running down the
   street in a sweat suit
but in a long coat
that interferes with his running:
because we are uneasy;
and then see
while leaning out the train window
how the cross-country runner is waving to us:
as a sign
that we're again without a care in the world—

Feeling awkward transforms itself into a green traffic
   signal
toward which we are walking
while it is still green
and the yellow signal

auf die wir zulaufen
schaltet um auf das Schaufenster eines
                              Lebensmittelladens
an einem Feiertag
und im leeren Lebensmittelladen verwandelt sich die
Wurstschneidemaschine in einen vollbesetzten Lift
in dem wir mit zu Boden geschlagenen Augen fahren
wenn wir verlegen sind –:

Nennen wir also die Schuldlosigkeit
Nagelschuh
die Ratlosigkeit
Hotelzimmer
die Ausweglosigkeit
neun Uhr
die Unschlüssigkeit
eine stehende Rolltreppe
die Scham
einen vollbesetzten Lift
und die Geduld
eine Platzanweiserin im Kino
die im Finstern mit einer Schachtel zwischen den
                              Händen
neben der Leinwand wartet
bis das junge Mädchen auf der Leinwand
die Ware angeboten hat
die die ältliche Platzanweiserin
voll Scham
wenn es hell geworden ist
als wäre sie in einem vollbesetzten Lift
jetzt uns anbieten wird

toward which we rush
switches over to the display window of the grocery store
on a holiday
and in the empty grocery store the meat slicing machine
    transforms itself
into a fully loaded elevator in which we ride with lowered
    eyes when we
feel awkward—:

So let us agree to call innocence
shoe nails
perplexity
hotel room
inescapability
nine o'clock
indecisiveness
a stationary escalator
self-consciousness
a crowded elevator
and patience
the usherette in a movie house
waiting in the dark near the screen
with a tray in her hands
until the girl on-screen
has offered the merchandise
which the elderly usherette
quite self-consciously
when the house lights come on
as though she was in a crowded elevator
will now offer to us

oder umgekehrt
oder umgekehrt –

Wir betreten unser Bewußtsein:
wie in einem Märchen ist es dort früher Morgen
auf einer Wiese im Frühsommer:
wenn wir neugierig sind;
wie in einem Western ist es dort Mittag
mit einer großen ruhigen Hand auf der Theke:
wenn wir gespannt sind;
wie in einem Tatsachenbericht über einen Lustmord
ist es dort früher Nachmittag
in einem schwülen Spätsommer
in einer Scheune:
wenn wir ungeduldig sind;
wie in einer Rundfunknachricht
überschreiten dort gegen Abend fremde Truppen die
                                                    Grenze:
wenn wir verwirrt sind;
und wie in der tiefen Nacht
wenn ein Ausgehverbot verhängt ist
breitet sich dort die Stille der Straßen aus
wenn wir uns vor niemandem äußern können –

Jemand sieht so viele Gegenstände
daß ihm die Gegenstände gleichgültig werden –
jemand sieht so viele gleichgültige Gegenstände
daß er nach und nach sich selber aus dem Bewußtsein
                                                    verliert –
dann sieht er einen Gegenstand
den er *nicht* sehen will

or vice versa
or vice versa—

We enter our consciousness:
as in a fairy tale it is early morning there
on a meadow in early summer:
when we are curious;
as in a Western it is noon there
with a large calm hand resting on the bar:
when we are tense;
as in a factual report about a sex crime
it is early afternoon there
on a muggy late summer day
in a barn:
when we are impatient;
as in a radio news report
foreign troops are crossing the border toward evening:
when we are confused;
and as in the dead of night
when there is a curfew
the stillness of the streets begins to spread
when we can't say a word before anyone—

Someone sees so many objects
he becomes indifferent to them—
someone sees so many indifferent objects
he gradually loses himself out of his consciousness—
then he sees an object
which he does *not* want to see

oder den er gern *länger* sehen möchte
oder den er gern *haben* möchte
so daß der Gegenstand ein Gegenstand
seiner Schaulust
seines Willens
seines Unwillens wird
und er ihn *anschaut*
oder ihn *abwehrt*
oder ihn *haben* will:
und er kommt zu Bewußtsein –

Erst als der Angeklagte verurteilt wird
erkennen wir
daß der Verurteilte angeklagt war

or which he would like to see *more* of
or which he would like to *have*
so that the object becomes an object
with which he would like to pander to the desire of his eyes
an object
of his will
of his ill-will
and he *regards* it
or *rejects* it
or wants to *have* it
and he becomes conscious—

Only when the defendant is sentenced
do we realize
that the defendant was accused.

Die Farbenlehre

In M. ist ein Kind von einem Unbekannten im Auto
mitgenommen und später mit einem Hammer auf
den Kopf geschlagen worden:

Der Junge sagt,
er sei von einem Mann in einem GRÜNEN
Auto mitgenommen und mit einem Hammer mit
ROTEM
Griff geschlagen worden.
Um auf der Toilette auszutreten, sei er mit dem
Mann in eine Wirtschaft gegangen, in der die
männlichen Angestellten ROTE
Jacken und SCHWÄRZLICHE
Hosen getragen hätten,
und in der Toilette habe eine Frau mit WEISSEN
Haaren gesessen und an GRAUEN
oder BRAUNEN
Socken gestrickt.
Der Mann habe sich mit einer ROSA
Seife die Hände gewaschen,
und in der Wirtschaft sei ein DURCHSICHTIGES
Regal gewesen, in dem GOLDENE
Nüsse und GELBE
Kartoffelchips ausgestellt waren.
Der Mann habe ihm GELBE

Color Theory

In M. a stranger in a car kidnapped a child and later hit it
over the head with a hammer:

    The boy says
    he was taken along by a man in a GREEN
    car and beaten with a hammer with a RED
    handle:
    To go to the toilet the man took him to a restaurant
    in which the male employees wore RED
    jackets and BLACKISH
    pants,
    and in the toilet sat a woman with WHITE
    hair who was knitting GRAY
    or BROWN
    socks.
    The man washed his hands with PINK
    soap,
    and in the restaurant there was a TRANSPARENT
    shelf with GOLDEN
    nuts
    and YELLOW
    potato chips on display.
    The man bought him YELLOW

Limonade gekauft und im Auto,
um ihn zum Lachen zu bringen,
eine GRÜNE
Luftmatratze aufgeblasen und ihn in einen Neubau
                                    geführt
und dort vor einer WEISSEN
Wand ziemlich lange die Notdurft verrichtet.
Der Mann habe einen Hut mit einem SILBERNEN
Abzeichen getragen, das an den Rändern SCHWARZ
gewesen sei, und habe in einem ROTEN
Haus den Hammer mit dem ROTEN
Griff geholt und sei sehr groß gewesen und habe ihn
mit ziemlich HELLEN
Augen FINSTER
angeschaut:

Aristoteles sagte, den Zustand des Raums um uns,
wenn wir mit offenen gesunden Augen keine Gegenstände erblickten, nennten wir FINSTERNIS,
und Goethe (sagte), wir sähen das einfache GRÜN
einer frisch gemähten Wiese mit Zufriedenheit, ob
es gleich nur eine unbedeutende Fläche sei, und ein
Wald tue in einiger Entfernung schon als große
EINFÖRMIGE Masse unserem Auge wohl:

Der Mann habe ihm versprochen, er gehe mit ihm
auf eine Wiese, um dort Maulwürfe zu fangen,
und in den Wald, um dort Hasen zu schießen: sagt
das Kind.
Auf dem Weg in den Wald seien sie an einer

lemonade and in the car,
to make him laugh,
blew up a GREEN
air mattress and led him into a building under construction
and there in front of a WHITE
wall he relieved himself rather lengthily.
The man, the boy says, was wearing a hat with a SILVER
badge whose edges were BLACK
and in a RED
house he got the hammer with the RED
handle and was very big
and gave him a DARK
look
out of rather BRIGHT
eyes:

Aristotle said what we call darkness is that condition of
space about us when we regard it with open, unimpaired
eyes and see no objects, and Goethe (said) we look at the
simple GREEN of a meadow with satisfaction, though it
might only represent an insignificant patch, and a forest
gives our eyes pleasure even at some distance as a large
UNIFORM mass:

The man promised to take him to the meadow to catch
moles, and into the woods to shoot rabbits: says the child.
On the way to the woods they passed a gutter pipe

Dachrinne vorbeigekommen, unter der das Pflaster
SCHWARZ
gewesen sei,
und auf einer Wiese habe sich der Mann mit einem
GELBEN
Kamm, den er einer ebenso GELBEN
Plastikhülle entnommen habe,
die Haare hinter die Ohren gekämmt,
und am Waldrand habe ein Strauch mit ziemlich
SCHWARZEN
Knospen gestanden.
Im Wald habe es der Mann VIOLETTES
Wasser in einem Baumloch riechen lassen und ihm
unter einem Gebüsch, weil es schneite, BUNTE
Heiligenbilder gezeigt und sei mit ihm über einen
SCHWARZEN
Bach gesprungen und habe ihm im Dickicht eine
ROTE
Narbe am Bauch
und ein WEISSES
Stecktuch
und in einer Baumwurzel die Reste eines Vogels
mit GELBEM
Schnabel
und eine SCHIMMERNDE
Haarspange
und im Finstern eine LEUCHTENDE
Armbanduhr gezeigt
und habe ROTE
Sockenhalter getragen,
die das Kind gesehen habe,

the pavement beneath which was BLACK,
and on the meadow
the man combed his hair with a YELLOW
comb which he extracted from a plastic case
which was just as YELLOW
and at the edge of the forest stood a bush
with rather BLACK
buds.
In the woods the man let him smell VIOLET
water in a tree hole and under a bush,
because it was snowing, he showed him COLORFUL
pictures of saints, and jumped with him across a BLACK
brook, and in the thicket showed him a RED
scar on his stomach
and a small WHITE
rubber sheet
and in the root of a tree the remains of a bird with a
    YELLOW
beak
and a GLINTING
hair pin
and in the DARKNESS
a GLOWING
wristwatch
and was wearing RED
sock suspenders
which the boy says he saw

sooft sich der Mann hinhockte und sich im SCHNEE
die FLECKIGEN
Finger abwusch:

Das Kind hat die Schuhe verloren. Es handelt sich
um Halbschuhe Größe 28, SCHWARZ

whenever the man squatted down
to wash his SPLOTCHY
hands in the SNOW:

The child has lost his shoes. They are size 6, BLACK.

Einige Alternativen in der indirekten Rede

TATEN seien die Alternativen zu WORTEN
so wie ICH die Alternative zu IHM sei
oder wie WIR die Alternative zur UNTERDRÜCKUNG
                                seien
oder wie DU die Alternative zur LEEREN WOHNUNG
                                seist:

WORTE wieder, sagt man, seien die Alternative
                        zum DENKEN
so wie VERHANDLUNGEN die Alternative zum KRIEG
                                seien
oder wie der WIRKLICHKEITSSINN die Alternative
                  zum UNVERBINDLICHEN SPIEL sei
oder wie die SCHÄDLINGSBEKÄMPFUNG die Alternative
                  zum KARTOFFELKÄFER sei:

DAS DENKEN wieder soll, berichtet man, die
                Alternative zu den TATEN sein
so wie DIE STICKIGE LUFT eine Alternative zu denen
              sein soll, DIE FÜR REINE LUFT SORGEN
oder wie DIE ANARCHIE die Alternative zum GUTEN
            WILLEN ALLER BETEILIGTEN sein soll
oder wie die Alternative zum KLEINEN FINGER GAR
                  NICHTS sein soll:

Several Alternatives for Indirect Discourse

ACTIONS are said to be the alternatives to WORDS
just as I is said to be the alternative to HIM
or as WE is said to be the alternative to SURPRESSION
or as YOU are said to be the alternative to the EMPTY APART-
   MENT:

Yet WORDS, so they say, are also the alternative to THINKING
just as NEGOTIATIONS are the alternative to WAR
or as the SENSE OF REALITY is the alternative to PLAYING
   AROUND
or as PEST CONTROL is the alternative to the COLORADO BEETLE:

Yet THINKING, so they report, is supposed to be the alternative to ACTIONS
just as STUFFY AIR is supposed to be the alternative to those
WHO MAKE SURE THE AIR IS CLEAN
or as ANARCHY is supposed to be the alternative to the
GOOD WILL OF ALL MEN
or as the alternative to the LITTLE FINGER is supposed to be
NOTHING AT ALL:

Die Alternativen, könnte man also sagen, stellten
                    zwei Worte zur Wahl /
die Alternativen bestünden aus Worten /
die Worte behaupteten, schon als Worte, was
                    SEIN SOLLE /
die Alternativen stellten zwei Worte zur Wahl, von
denen eines SEIN SOLLE, damit das andre NICHT SEI /
die Alternativen stellten sich als Worte zur Wahl, die
dadurch, daß Worte, schon als Worte, behaupteten,
was SEIN SOLLE, schon zwischen zwei Worten keine
                    Wahl mehr zuließen /
wenn WORTE die Alternative zum DENKEN wären,
wie die Alternativen, die WORTE seien, behaupteten,
weil sie WORTE seien (und Worte *behaupteten*), –
so wären die Alternativen, die, schon als WORTE, behaupteten, was SEIN SOLLE, die geeignete Schädlings-
                    bekämpfung der GEDANKEN:

PARIER oder KREPIER!

Thus you could say that the alternatives presented a choice between two words/
the alternatives consisted of words/
the words as such already stated what OUGHT TO BE/
the alternatives presented a choice between two words of which one word OUGHT TO BE so that the other OUGHT NOT TO BE/
the alternatives presented themselves as a choice among words which, by means of the fact that words as such already stated WHAT OUGHT TO BE, no longer left a choice even among two words/
if WORDS were the alternative to THINKING, as the alternatives which are words are said to have stated because they are words (and words *did state*)—in that case the alternatives which already stated as words what OUGHT TO BE would be the suitable PEST CONTROL for THOUGHTS:

DO or DIE!

Geschichtslügen

DASS
im Frühjahr das Gras neben den Eisenbahnschienen;
im Sommer der Wald in Kalifornien und an der
Côte d'Azur;
im Herbst die Kartoffelstauden;
im Winter Invaliden in ihren Betten;
das ganze Jahr über Tankwagenfahrer verbrennen;

DASS
der Operierte, kaum aus der Narkose erwacht,
schon wieder Witze reißt;
ledige Mütter in Häusern mit Gasheizung wohnen;
vor den Verfolgern im Radrennen die Bahnschranken
niedergehen;
die Bosse der COSA NOSTRA im Hinterzimmer sitzen;
der Absturz des Flugzeugs von einem Bauern auf
dem Feld beobachtet wird;

DASS
der Ringer ZEBRA KID, im Ring gefürchtet, privat
ein gutmütiger Riese ist;

DASS
NOBBY STILES, Verteidiger von Manchester United,
auf dem Fußballplatz gefürchtet, außerhalb des Fußballplatzes keiner Fliege etwas antun könnte;

Historical Lies

THAT

in spring the grass next to railroad tracks;
in summer the forests in California and on the Côte d'Azur
in fall the potato weeds;
in winter the invalids in their beds;
throughout the year drivers of gasoline trucks go up in
 flame;

THAT

the patient, as he comes out of anesthesia, is acting up
again;
unmarried mothers live in houses with gas heating;
railway crossing gates are lowered in front of the pursuers
in bicycle races;
cosa nostra bosses sit in back rooms;
the airplane crash is observed by a farmer on a field;

THAT

the wrestler ZEBRA KID is feared in the ring but is as gentle
as a lamb in private;

THAT

NOBBY STILES, fullback of Manchester United, is feared on
the soccer field but off the field couldn't harm a fly;

DASS
in den USA Eispickel Mordwerkzeuge sind;
die reiche Erbin kinderlos ist;
der Polizeispitzel feuchte Hände hat;
der Ehemann der Gebärenden vor dem Kreißsaal
auf und ab geht;
der Mörder des Taxifahrers ein Fahrgast mit dunkler
Hautfarbe ist;
die Sternschnuppen von Kurgästen bestaunt werden;
der KZ-Wächter ein Hundeliebhaber ist;
in Burma die Fähren kentern;
in Montenegro die Autobusse verunglücken;
in Buenos Aires die Fußballzuschauer einander
zertrampeln;

DASS
die geschändete Küchenhilfe auf einem Kohlenhaufen
im Keller hockt;
die Zapfer in den Stehbierhallen gewalttätig sind;
von Straßenbahnen vor allem die Rentner erfaßt
werden;
die Hilfsarbeiter mit russischen oder polnischen Namen in einer Kammer über dem Kuhstall wohnen;
die Straße, wenn der Lastwagen umstürzt, voller
Orangen ist;

DASS
der Sittenstrolch vor der Entlarvung als gutsituierter
Bürger mit guten Umgangsformen gegolten hat und
der Attentäter von seinem Arbeitgeber als fleißig /
gutmütig / unauffällig bezeichnet wird und der Hei-
ratsschwindler feingliedrige Hände hat;

THAT

icepicks are instruments of death in the u.s.;
the wealthy heiress has no children;
the private eye has clammy hands;
the husband of the woman in labor paces up and down
outside the delivery room;
the murderer of the taxi driver was a passenger with dark
skin;
falling stars are watched with wonderment by vacationers;
the KZ guard was fond of dogs;
the ferries capsize in Burma;
buses meet with misfortune in Montenegro;
the spectators of soccer games in Buenos Aires trample
each other to death;

THAT

the ravished kitchen help squats on a coal heap in the
cellar;
the servers in beer halls are violent and brutal;
street cars run over pensioners as a matter of course;
foreign workers with Russian and Polish surnames live in
hovels above the cowshed;
the street is filled with oranges when the truck overturns;

THAT

the sex fiend was considered a well-situated and well-
mannered citizen before he was unmasked and the assassin
is called zealous / discreet / good-natured by his employer
and the false suitor has delicate hands;

DASS

die Arbeiter beim Mittagsschlaf in der Betontrommel;
die alten Radfahrer auf dem Rad;
die verletzten Schifahrer auf dem Weg ins Tal;
die Kleinkinder in unbewachten Momenten sterben;

DASS

in Metz noch mit dem Fallbeil hingerichtet wird;

DASS

in Wochenendhäuschen eingebrochen wird;
der Erpresser am Telefon eine sanfte Stimme hat;
Vertreter den Fuß zwischen die Tür schieben;
Ertrunkene in Flüssen sofort abgetrieben werden;

DASS

die Kirschen Kerne haben;
daß gegen Abend der Wind weht;
daß die Hängematten hin und her schwingen;
daß die Wasserläufer übers Wasser laufen;
daß die Orgel Orgel spielt;
daß die bewegliche Habe beweglich ist;
daß Zahnlose zahnlos sind;
daß Straßen Wege sind;
daß Wege Wege sind;
daß Fischgräten Gräten sind;
daß Wörter wie »Gekreische« und »Lebkuchen«
       GEKREISCHE und LEBKUCHEN bedeuten –:
das alles –

THAT

the workers during their nap in the cement barrel;
the old bicyclists on their bicycles;
the injured skier on his way into the valley;
toddlers die in unguarded moments;

THAT

people are still guillotined in Metz;

THAT

weekend cottages are burglarized;
the blackmailer's telephone voice is gentle;
salesmen shove their feet between doors;
the drowned are immediately swept out to sea;

THAT

cherries have stones;
that there is always a breeze toward evening;
that hammocks swing back and forth;
that water striders stride across water;
that the organ plays organ;
that moveable goods are moveable;
the toothless are toothless;
that streets are ways;
that ways are ways;
that words like 'ruckus' and 'gefilte fish' mean RUCKUS and
GEFILTE FISH—:
that everything—

das ist alles –
das alles ist alles –
das alles ist alles nicht alles nicht wahr.

Denn die Zapfer in den Stehbierhallen sind
    Heiratsschwindler mit feingliedrigen Händen.
Denn die Augenzeugen des abstürzenden Flugzeugs
                    sind Kurgäste.
Denn die Arbeiter sterben auf Kohlenhaufen
            im Keller.

that is everything—
that everything is everything—
that everything is everything is not at all true.

For the servers in beer halls are false suitors with delicate
hands.
For eye-witnesses of plane crashes are vacationers at spas.
For the workers expire on the coalheaps in the cellar.

Die japanische Hitparade vom 25. Mai 1968

1
HANA NO KUBIZAKARI/GINGA NO ROMANCE
Tigers

2
KOI NO SHIZUKU
Ito Yukari

3
MASSACHUSETTS
Bee Gees

4
YUBE NO HIMITSU
Ogawa Tomoko

5
KAMISAMA ONEGAI
Tempters

6
KANASHIKUTE YARIKIRENAI (UNBEARABLE SAD)
Folk Crusade

The Japanese Hit Parade of May 25, 1968

1

HANA NO KUBIZAKARI/GINGA NO ROMANCE
Tigers

2

KOI NO SHIZUKU
Ito Yukari

3

MASSACHUSETTS
Bee Gees

4

YUBE NO HIMITSU
Ogawa Tomoko

5

KAMISAMA ONEGAI
Tempters

6

KANASHIKUTE YARIKERENAI (UNBEARABLE SAD)
Folk Crusade

15

Satsuma no Hito
Kitajima Saburo

16

Valleri
Monkees

17

Ano Toki Kima wa Wawakatta
Spiders

18

Love Is Blue (L'Amour est bleu)
Paul Mariat

19

Daydream Believer
Monkees

20

Amairo no Kami no Otome (On the Windy Hill)
Village Singers

Veränderungen im Lauf des Tages

Solange ich noch allein bin, bin ich noch ich allein.
Solange ich noch unter Bekannten bin, bin ich noch
           ein Bekannter.
  Sobald ich aber unter Unbekannte komme –

Sobald ich auf die Straße trete – tritt ein Fußgänger
           auf die Straße.
Sobald ich in die Straßenbahn einsteige – steigt ein
           Fahrgast in die Straßenbahn.
Sobald ich das Juweliergeschäft betrete – betritt
           ein Herr das Juweliergeschäft.
Sobald ich den Einkaufswagen durch den Selbst-
bedienungsladen schiebe – schiebt ein Kunde den Ein-
kaufswagen durch den Selbstbedienungsladen.
Sobald ich das Warenhaus betrete – betritt ein
           Kauflustiger das Warenhaus.

Dann gehe ich an Kindern vorbei – und die Kinder
sehen einen Erwachsenen, der an ihnen vorbeigeht.
Dann betrete ich die Sperrzone – und die Wächter
sehen einen Unbefugten, der die Sperrzone betritt.
Dann sehe ich in der Sperrzone die Kinder vor mir
davonlaufen – und ich werde ein Wächter, vor dem
die Kinder davonlaufen, weil sie in der Sperrzone
           Unbefugte sind.

Changes during the Course of the Day

As long as I am still alone, I am still alone.
As long as I am still among acquaintances, I am still an acquaintance.
  But as soon as I am among strangers —

As soon as I step out on the street — a pedestrian steps out on the street.
As soon as I enter the subway — a subway rider enters the subway.
As soon as I enter the jewelry shop — a gentleman enters the jewelry shop.
As soon as I push the shopping cart through the super-market — a customer pushes the cart through the super-market.
As soon as I enter the department store — someone on a shopping spree enters the department store.

Then I walk past some children — and the children see an adult walking past. Then I enter the off-limits zone — and the guards see a trespasser enter the off-limits zone. Then I see children running away from me in the off-limits zone — and I become a guard whom the children flee because they are unauthorized persons in an off-limits zone.

Dann sitze ich in den Vorzimmern als Antragsteller.
Dann schreibe ich meinen Namen auf die Rückseite
                    des Briefes als Absender.
Dann fülle ich den Gutschein aus als ein vom Glück
                    Begünstigter.

Sobald ich dann nach dem »Schwarzen Weg« gefragt
                    werde – werde ich ein Ortskundiger.
Sobald ich dann das Unglaubliche sehe – werde ich
                    ein Zeuge.
Sobald ich dann die Kirche betrete – werde ich ein
                    Laie.
Sobald ich dann bei dem Unfall nicht weitergehe –
                    werde ich ein Neugieriger.
Sobald ich dann den »Schwarzen Weg« nicht kenne –
bin ich wieder einer, der den »Schwarzen Weg« nicht
                    kennt.

Kaum nehme ich dann die Mahlzeit ein – schon
                    kann ich sagen: Wir Verbraucher!
Kaum wird mir dann etwas gestohlen – schon
                    kann ich sagen: Wir Eigentümer!
Kaum gebe ich dann die Todesanzeige auf – schon
                    kann ich sagen: Wir Leidtragenden!
Kaum betrachte ich dann das Weltall – schon
                    kann ich sagen: Wir Menschen!

Ich lese den Roman in der Illustrierten – und werde
                    Einer unter Millionen.
Ich erfülle die Pflichten der Obrigkeit gegenüber
                    nicht – und schon bin ich ein Staatsbürger.

Then I sit in the waiting room as an applicant. Then I write my name on the back of the envelope as a sender. Then I fill out the lottery ticket as a winner.

As soon as I am asked how one gets to BLACK ROAD — I become someone who knows his way around town.
As soon as I see the incredible — I become a witness.
As soon as I enter the church — I become a layman.
As soon as I don't ignore an accident — I become a busybody.
As soon as I don't know how to get to BLACK ROAD — I am again someone who doesn't know his way to BLACK ROAD.

I have just consumed the meal — already I can say: We consumers!
I have just had something stolen from me — already I can say: We proprietors!
I have just placed the obituary — already I can say: We mourners!
I have just begun to contemplate the universe — already I can say: We human beings!

I read the novel in the mass publication — and become one among millions.
I don't fulfill my duties toward the authorities — and am no longer a dutiful citizen of the state.

Ich laufe bei dem Auflauf nicht davon – und schon
                              bin ich ein Aufrührer.
Ich schaue von dem Roman auf und betrachte die
Schönheit mir gegenüber – und wir werden Zwei
                              unter Millionen.

Dann steigt jemand aus dem fahrenden Zug nicht
                              aus – jemand? – Ein Reisender.
Dann spricht jemand ohne Akzent – jemand? –
                              Ein Inländer.
Dann hat jemand ein Gegenüber – und wird ein
                              Gegenüber.
Dann spielt jemand nicht mehr nur mit sich selber –
                              und wird ein Gegner.

Dann wird jemand in einer Stube der Stubenälteste.
Dann kriecht jemand aus einem Gebüsch im Park
                              und wird ein verdächtiges Subjekt.
Dann wird aus jemandem, über den gesprochen wird,
                              ein Gesprächsgegenstand.
Dann wird jemand auf einem Foto erkannt – und
                              wird ein X.
Dann ergeht sich jemand auf dem freien Land –
                              jemand? Ein Wanderer.

Als dann plötzlich vor mir ein Auto bremst – bin
                              ich ein Hindernis.
Dann werde ich im Dunkeln von einer Gestalt
            gesehen – und werde eine Gestalt im Dunkeln.
Als ich dann durch den Feldstecher beobachtet
                              werde – bin ich ein Objekt.

I don't run away during the riot — and I'm an inciter of riots.
I look up from the novel I'm reading and observe the beauty opposite me — and we become two among millions.

Then someone does not leave the moving train — someone? — A traveler.
Then someone speaks without an accent — someone? — A native.
Then someone has a vis-à-vis — and becomes a vis-à-vis.
Then someone no longer only plays by himself — and becomes an opponent.

Then someone crawls out from under a thicket in the park and becomes a suspicious subject.
Then someone who is being discussed becomes an object of discussion.
Then someone is recognized on a photo — and becomes an X.
Then someone takes a walk in the country — someone? A wanderer.

And when the car makes a sudden stop in front of me — I become an obstacle.
Then I am seen by a figure in the dark — and become a figure in the dark.
And when I am then observed through binoculars — I am an object.

Dann stolpert man über mich – und ich werde ein
                                        Körper.
Als man dann auf mich tritt – bin ich etwas Weiches.
Dann werde ich in etwas eingehüllt – und werde
                                        ein Inhalt.

Dann erkennt man, daß hier ein Barfüßiger über den
Feldweg gelaufen ist und daß ein Rechtshänder den
Schuß abgefeuert haben muß und daß einer mit der
Blutgruppe o hier gelegen hat und daß ich, nach der
Schäbigkeit des Aussehens zu schließen, ein Ausländer
sein muß.

Sobald man mich dann anruft – bleibt der Angerufene
                                        auf Anruf nicht stehen.
Sobald ich dann weit genug weg von den Beobachtern
                                        bin – ist das Objekt nur noch ein Punkt.
Sobald dann ich als Beobachter einen anrufe – bin
ich für den Angerufenen ein ganz schöner Schrecken.

Dann, endlich, treffe ich einen Bekannten – und
                                        zwei Bekannte treffen einander.
Dann, endlich, werde ich alleingelassen – und einer
                                        bleibt allein zurück.
Dann, endlich, bin ich allein – und einer ist mit sich
                                        allein.
Dann, schließlich, setze ich mich zu einem ins Gras –
                                        und bin endlich ein andrer.

Then someone stumbles over me — and I become a body.
And when I am then stepped upon — I become something soft.
Then I am wrapped up in something — and become a content.

Then one notices that someone has run barefoot over the dirt road and that a right-hander has fired the shot and that someone whose blood group is O has lain there and that I, judging by my shabby looks, must be a foreigner.

As soon as someone challenges me then — the one who's been challenged doesn't stop when challenged.
As soon as I am then far enough away from the observers — the object is nothing but a dot.
As soon as I, as an observer, challenge someone — I give the one who has been challenged quite a fright.

Then, finally, I meet an acquaintance — and two acquaintances meet.
Then, finally, I am left alone — and a single person remains behind alone.
Then, finally, I sit down next to someone in the grass — and am finally someone else.

Frankensteins Monsters Monster Frankenstein

Ah!
Unter dem Stroh im Stall liegt Frankensteins Monster.
In Carlsbrunn wohnt ein Doktor namens Stein.
Frankensteins Tochter fährt in der Kutsche zur Kur
                nach Insbad (oder nach Inzbad).
Die Burschen im Dorf heißen Fritz, Karl, Otto
                                und Hans.
Im Stall über dem Stroh hängt ein ziemlich schwarzer
                           Reifen aus Holz.
Der Pförtner ist das erste Opfer des Monsters, das
                   zweite Opfer heißt Gerda.
Im Stall unterm Stroh liegt Frankenstein,
                  Frankensteins Monster.

Im Herrschaftshaus spielt das Quartett einen echt
englischen Komponisten, aber auf Wunsch der Dame
                 des Hauses folgt Händel darauf.
Im Wirtshaus sind die Tischtücher so weißblau
            kariert, daß man Heimweh kriegt.
Im Keller nimmt der Doktor dem erschrockenen
         Assistenten den Handschuh aus der Hand.
Es gibt auch eine Stadt namens Frankenstein.
Im Wald schläft Frankensteins Monster weinend
               unter dem Farnkraut.

Frankenstein's Monster's
Monster Frankenstein

Ah!
Under the straw in the stable lies Frankenstein's monster.
In Carlsbrunn lives a doctor named Stein.
Frankenstein's daughter takes the coach to the baths in
Insbad (or Inzbad).
The guys in the village are called Fritz, Karl, Otto and
Hans.
Above the straw in the stable hangs a wooden hoop which
is quite black.
The doorman is the monster's first victim, the second
victim is called Gerda.
In the stable under the straw lies Frankenstein, Franken-
stein's monster.

In the manor house the quartet is playing a genuinely
English composer, but the lady of the manor insists and
he is followed by Handel.
In the village inn the tablecloths are checkered the kind
of white and blue that makes you homesick.
In the cellar the doctor takes the glove from the hand of
the startled assistant.
There is also a town called Frankenstein.
In the woods Frankenstein's monster is weeping in his
sleep under the ferns.

Der Geliebte von Frankensteins Tochter heißt Hans.
Frankensteins Monster steht auf dem Altan des
Herrschaftshauses.
Der Doktor Stein macht eine Krankenvisite.
Das Liebespaar heißt Gerda und Franz, sitzt mitten
in der Nacht unterm Gebüsch und zählt Ameisen.
Der Stallknecht hängt im Stall an einem ziemlich
schwarzen Reifen aus Holz.
Frankensteins Monster hieß früher Hans.

Der Schrei der Dame des Hauses löscht die Kerze für
die Partitur des Streichquartetts aus.
Frankensteins Monster hat sich unter das Farnkraut
verkrochen.
Frankensteins Tochter trug einen Reifrock aus Inzbad
(oder aus Insbad).
Hans und Frankensteins Tochter saßen oft miteinan-
der im Gras und aßen aus dem Jausenkorb, der zwischen ihnen im Gras stand.
Die Dame des Hauses hat einen Fächer zwischen
Daumen und Fingern.
Frankensteins Monster, in seiner Verzweiflung,
hat den Hemdkragen offen.

»Ihr seid so gut zu mir!« sagte Hans.
Der Mann aus dem Volke reibt sich den Bauch.
»Ich bin immer nur angestarrt worden!« sagt
Frankensteins Monster.
Der Doktor Stein heißt jetzt Doktor Franck und hat
eine Praxis in London West, Harley Street.

Frankenstein's daughter's lover is called Hans.
Frankenstein's monster is standing on the manor house balcony.
Doctor Stein is making a sick call.
The lovers, who are called Gerda and Franz, are sitting in the bushes around midnight counting ants.
The stable boy is hanging in the stable from a wooden hoop which is quite black.
Frankenstein's monster used to be called Hans.

The lady of the manor screams, extinguishing the candle that had illuminated the string quartet score.
Frankenstein's monster has crawled under the ferns.
Frankenstein's daughter was wearing a hoopskirt from Inzbad (or Insbad).
Hans and Frankenstein's daughter often sat together in the grass eating from the picnic basket between them in the grass.
The lady of the manor is holding a fan between index finger and thumb.
Frankenstein's monster, in his despair, has his shirt collar open.

"You are so good to me," says Hans.
One of the villagers is rubbing his stomach.
"People always stared at me," says Frankenstein's monster.
Doctor Stein is now called Doctor Franck and has a practice in Harley Street, London West.

Die unbenutzten Todesursachen

Indem ich mit mir selber wette, betrete ich blindlings
den Liftschacht – aber der Aufzug ist da: habe ich die
Wette verloren?
Ich lasse es darauf ankommen und gehe im Herbst
durch den Wald – aber die Treibjagd ist schon zuende:
auf was habe ich es ankommen lassen?
Ich nehme mich zusammen und gehe über die Straße –
aber alle Fahrzeuge fahren an mir vorbei: welchen
Sinn hatte es, daß ich mich zusammennahm?

Wenn ich im Fleischerladen bin, gelten die Beilhiebe
nicht mir.
Wenn ich die Starkstromleitung berühre, trage ich
Schuhe mit Gummisohlen.
Wenn ich mich aus dem Fenster beuge, ist die
Brüstung zu hoch.
Wenn ich stolpere, stolpere ich auf dem Erdboden.
Wenn ich falle, falle ich glücklich.
Wenn ich auf dem Gerüst stehe, ist das morsche Brett
schon entfernt worden.
Wenn ich mit der Schußwaffe spiele, sind meine
Finger zu ruhig.
Wenn ich auf die Schlange trete, ist die Schlange
schon tot:

Unused Opportunities

Making a bet with myself, I take a blind step into the elevator shaft — but the elevator is there: did I lose the bet? I take a chance and walk through the woods in fall — but the hunting season is over: what did I take a chance on? I get a grip on myself and cross the street — but all vehicles drive past me: what was the point of getting a grip on myself?

When I'm in the butcher shop the hacking blows of the meat cleaver are not meant for me. When I touch the high tension wire I wear shoes with rubber soles. When I bend out of the window the window sill is much too high. When I trip I trip on level ground. When I fall it is a lucky fall. When I stand on the scaffolding the rotten board has been replaced. When I play with firearms my fingers never tremble. When I step on the snake the snake is dead:

Es nützt nichts, daß ich in kochendes Wasser falle –
es ist nur ein Traum.
Es schadet nichts, daß ich von Kannibalen gegessen
werde – ich bin nur die Figur eines Witzes.
Es tut nichts zur Sache, daß mir der Kopf von einem
Gorilla abgebissen wird – ich bin nur der Held einer
Geschichte.

Während die Stricknadel unbenutzt im Wollknäuel
steckt,
während die Rasierklinge unbenutzt neben dem
Waschbecken liegt,
während das Pflaster unbenutzt tief genug unter mir
liegt,
während der Lastwagen unbenutzt gegen die Mauer
zurückstößt,
während die Tür des Kühlschranks unbenutzt zufällt,
während die tödliche Dosis unbenutzt dort im
Schrank steht,
während anderswo unbenutzt tödliche Kälte herrscht,
während anderswo Feuer unbenutzt niederbrennt,
während Felsblöcke woanders aufschlagen,
während
zum Töten Ermächtigte woanders andere töten,
während nicht zum Töten Ermächtigte woanders
andere töten,
während andere zum Töten Ermächtigte woanders
andere zum Getötetwerden Verpflichtete töten und
während woanders andere zum Getötetwerden Verpflichtete andere zum Töten Ermächtigte töten,

It's no use my falling into boiling water — it only happens in a dream.
It's harmless my being devoured by cannibals — I'm merely the figure in a joke.
It's inconsequential that a gorilla bites off my head — I'm only the hero of a story.

While the knitting needle sticks unused in the ball of wool,
while the razor blade lies unused next to the washbasin,
while the pavement is lying unused far enough below,
while the truck uselessly backs up against the wall,
while the icebox door falls shut uselessly,
while the deadly dose stands unused in the closet,
while some place else deadly cold reigns uselessly,
while some place else fires are raging without its being any
    use at all,
while rocks are falling somewhere else without its being
    any use,
while
those empowered to kill are killing others someplace else,
while others who are not empowered to kill are killing
others someplace else,
while others who are empowered to kill someplace else are
killing others who are bound to be killed and while someplace else others who are bound to be killed are killing
others who are empowered to kill,

während
Messerspitzen,
Axtschneiden,
Gammastrahlen,
scharfkantige Steine,
rasende Eisenbahnen,
Straßenwalzen,
Gletscherspalten,
rotierende Propeller,
Treibsand,
giftige Pilze,
giftiger Schimmel,
tödliche Spinnen auf Bananen,
flüssiger Stahl,
Minenfelder,
kochendes Pech,
ausströmendes Gas,
tiefes Wasser
unbenutzt sind,

stehe ich hier, auf *meinem* Platz,

einen Schritt zu weit weg von der Bananenschale,
mehr Schritte zu weit weg vom rotierenden Propeller,
noch mehr Schritte zu weit weg von der Spitze des
       Holzpflocks, der in die Erde gerammt wird,
noch mehr Schritte zu weit weg von der Spitze des
       Brieföffners, der neben mir liegt,
am meisten Schritte zu weit weg vom Liftschacht, der
leer ist –

while
knifepoints
ax edges
gamma rays
sharp-edged stones,
speeding trains,
steam rollers,
glacial fissures,
rotating propellers,
drifting sand,
poison mushrooms,
poisonous mold,
deadly spiders on bananas,
molten steel,
mine fields,
boiling tar,
escaping gas,
deep water,
remain unused

I stand right here, on *my* spot,

one step too far from the banana peel,
several steps too far from the rotating propeller,
several more steps too far from the wooden peg that is
being rammed
into the ground,
several more steps too far from the tip of the letter opener
that lies
over there,
most of all: far too many steps from the empty elevator
shaft —

und atme nicht ein
und atme nicht aus
und rühre mich nicht vom Fleck.

and don't inhale
and don't exhale
and don't move from the spot.

Vergleiche für nichts Vergleichbares

Wie
  Wie
        ein
    Wie
        der Brunnenmacher
      Wie
        das Schild GÖSSER BIER im Horrorfilm:

Wie
  Wie
        ein
    Wie
        die Hausbewohner, die in der Kirche sind,
        als das Flugzeug aufs Haus stürzt wie
        der Spalt im Stroh, in dem der Flüchtige,
        nachdem er sich in die Scheune verkrochen
        hatte, eingesunken: dann eingebrochen: dann
        erstickt ist wie
        die Zugfenster, die, nachdem sie, als der Zug
        auf offener Strecke anhielt, heruntergescho-
        ben worden sind, jetzt, als der Zug wieder
        anfährt, nach und nach wieder hinaufgescho-
        ben werden:

Comparisons for What's Incomparable

Like
  Like
      a
   Like
    the well digger
   Like
    the sign Gösser Beer in the horror film:
Like
  Like
      a
  Like
      the family that prays together in church when
      the plane crashes into their home like
      the gap in the straw through which the refugee
      slowly slides after he had hidden in the barn:
      then broke in: then suffocated like
      the train windows which are pushed down when
      the train stops on an open stretch and are pushed
      up bit by bit when the train gets underway again:

Wie
  Wie
      man
    Wie
       wenn man im Sturm weit weg ein Kind über
die Straße laufen sieht
und zugleich im Hotelzimmer nebenan das
Flüstern eines Mannes und dann das Lachen
der Frau hört
und zugleich Leimrinnsale von frischgekleb-
ten Plakaten auf den Gehsteig tropfen sieht
und zugleich sieht, wie jemand allein am
Tisch sitzen bleibt, während seine Begleiterin,
um sich frisch zu machen, hinausgeht
und zugleich den Angeklagten das Gesicht in
die Hand verstecken sieht:

Wie
  Wie
    wenn
      Wie wenn man in der Eisernen Jungfrau
                 einatmen möchte
und dann aufwacht und sieht die Wände
                    schwitzen
und dann den Lidstrich trocknen sieht
und sieht dann eine Schwangere am
                Brückengeländer:

wie das Fett auf dem Boden des
                Grillautomaten
wie Milch in den Straßenbahnschienen

Like
  Like
       one
    Like
      when you see a child run across the street from
      far away during a storm and, simultaneously, in
      the adjacent hotel room hear a man whispering
      and simultaneously see rivulets of glue dripping
      onto the sidewalk from freshly pasted-up posters
      and simultaneously see someone stay behind
      alone at his table while his girl goes out to put on
      fresh makeup
      and simultaneously see the defendant hide his
      face in his hands:

Like
  Like
   when
      Like when you want to inhale inside an iron
      maiden
      and then wake up and see the walls sweating
      and then see the makeup drying on the eyelids
      and then see a pregnant woman leaning over the
      railing of a bridge:

      like the grease in the tray of the rotary grill
      like milk in the streetcar tracks

wie das Augenzwinkern des Fernsehkochs
wie der Schatten des Kameramanns
wie die Innenstadt
wie das große G
wie:
»wie vor der Gewalt des Feuers ein Schwarm von
Heuschrecken ins Wasser klatscht und der Himmel
von dem Geschrei der Kraniche tönt und das Ge-
treide zermalmt wird vom Trott der brüllenden Rin-
der und vor dem ungeheuren Delphin fliehend die
anderen Fische in den Buchten sich tummeln und die
Schafe des reichen Mannes, ohne Unterlaß blökend,
zahllos in der Hürde die Eimer mit schäumender
Milch anfüllen und der Mann, der die Schlange er-
blickte, voll Entsetzen zurückfährt und die unzähl-
baren Scharen der Fliegen, wenn die Milch von der
Butter herabtrieft, rastlos das Gehege der ländlichen
Hirten im luftigen Frühling durchschwärmen und die
Zikaden, die auf den Bäumen sitzen, von ihren hel-
len Stimmen die Wälder erschwirren lassen«:
Wie:
 Wie
   5
  Wie
    4
   Wie
     3
    Wie
      2
     Wie
       1:
Wie wenn man ein Tuch über den Käfig wirft, um die
schreienden Vögel zum Schweigen zu bringen

like the cook that winks at you on the t.v. show
like midtown
like capital G
like:
"like a swarm of locusts slammed into the water by the
force of the fire and the sky resounding with the wailing
of cranes and the grain ground underfoot by the trampling
of a bellowing herd of cattle and the fish leaping over
one another in the coves as they flee the mammoth dolphin
and the rich man's sheep, bleating incessantly, in countless
numbers filling the buckets in the sheep fold with foam-
ing milk and the man drawing back in fright as he sees
the snake and the uncountable legions of flies swarming
restlessly through the enclosure of the rural herdsman in
the airy spring when the milk is dripping off the butter
and the crickets in the trees make the woods whir with
their shrill racket:"
Like:
  Like
      5
    Like
      4
    Like
      3
    Like
      2
    Like
      1:
Like throwing a sheet over the cage to silence the screech-
ing birds.

Unterscheidungen

»Dieses Geräusch kenne ich! Gerade ist jemand gestorben!«
– »Nein, es ist dir nur ein Heuschreck auf das Bett gehüpft.«

Kaum fange ich an, die Augen zu öffnen – schon fange ich an, Einzelheiten zu unterscheiden.

»Kennst du den Unterschied zwischen einer Schlange, die über einen Jausenkorb kriecht, und einem Hoteldiener, der mit dem Zimmermädchen vor dem Haus auf einem Hügel steht?« –
– »Dieses Geräusch kenne ich!« –
– »Nein, es ist nur eine Schlange über dein Bett gekrochen.«

»Viele schmutzige Handtücher liegen auf dem Boden.« –
– »Habe ich die Handtücher *wirklich* liegen sehen oder habe ich nur den Satz gelesen: ›Viele schmutzige Handtücher liegen auf dem Boden‹?« –
– »Ja, von den schmutzigen Handtüchern hast du nur geträumt.«

Kaum fange ich an zu schauen – schon muß ich hier und dort was erblicken: hier ein schmutziges Hand-

Distinctions

"I know that noise! Someone has just died!"
"No, it was just a grasshopper jumping on your bed."

Scarcely have I begun to open my eyes — already I begin
to distinguish one thing from another.

"Do you know the difference between a snake that crawls
over the picnic basket and a bellboy who stands with the
chambermaid in front of the house on the hill?" —
— "I know that noise!"
— "No, it was only a snake crawling over your bed."

"A lot of dirty towels are lying on the floor." —
— "Did I really see the towels lying there, or did I only
read the sentence: 'A lot of dirty towels are lying on the
floor'?" —
— "Yes, you only dreamed of the dirty towels."

Scarcely have I begun to look — already I am forced to
perceive something here and there: here a dirty towel on

tuch auf dem Boden, dort einen Jausenkorb mit einem Geschirrtuch darüber.

»Erinnerst du dich an das Geschirrtuch, mit dem du nach dem Heuschreck geschlagen hast?« –
– »Das war der Hoteldiener.«

Kaum fange ich an, Einzelheiten zu unterscheiden – schon muß ich mich erinnern.

»Früher schwang der Hoteldiener das *Geschirr*tuch, jetzt aber liegt ein *Hand*tuch auf dem Boden!« –
– »Ja, du hast dir die Hände im Geschirrtuch abgetrocknet.«

»Wie wird diese Bewegung genannt?« –
– »Wehen.« –
– »Also ist das, was sich da am Fenster bewegt, der Wind?« –
– »Nein, ein Vorhang bewegt sich.« –
– »Nein, der Wind bewegt einen Vorhang.«

Kaum fange ich an zu reden – schon nehme ich eine Tarnfarbe an und unterscheide mich nicht mehr von der Umgebung.

»Dieser Strick dient nicht zum Erhängen, sondern als Zahnseide.«

Kaum fange ich an zu unterscheiden – schon macht mich das Unterscheiden eins mit meiner Umgebung.

the floor, there a picnic basket with a dishtowel over it.

"Do you remember the dishtowel with which you swatted the grasshopper?" —
— "That was the bellboy."

Scarcely have I begun to distinguish among particulars — already I must recollect.

"At one time the bellboy was swatting with the *dish*towel, but now there's a *face*towel lying on the floor!" —
— "Yes, you dried your hands on the dishtowel."

"What is that movement called?" —
— "Blowing." —
— "So what is moving at the window is the wind?" —
— "No, a curtain is moving." —
— "No, the wind is moving the curtain."

Scarcely have I begun to speak — already I am camouflaged and no longer distinguishable from my surroundings.

"This cord is not the hangman's, but is dental floss."

Scarcely have I begun to distinguish — already differentiating makes me one with my surroundings.

»Wenn die Wilde Jagd kommt, legen wir uns auf einen Feldweg und bilden mit unseren Körpern ein Wagenrad.« –
– »Und wenn du allein bist?« –
– »Wenn ich allein bin, kommt keine Wilde Jagd.«

Kaum suche ich vergeblich nach einem Satz für etwas in der Umgebung – schon unterscheide ich mich schmerzhaft von der Umgebung.

»Kennst du den Unterschied zwischen jemandem, der in einiger Entfernung von dir in der Nacht mit einer Taschenlampe geht, und dem Heiligen Alexius unter der Stiege?« –
– »Diesen Anblick kenne ich! Jemand ist gerade gestorben!« –
– »Ja, du bist auf einen Pilz getreten, und der Pilz, beim Platzen hat er dich angestaubt.« –
– »Davon also sind die Handtücher schmutzig geworden!«

Kaum bin ich eins mit der Umgebung – schon fange ich wieder zu reden an und unterscheide mich.

»Ist es nicht der Tintenfisch, der eine Flüssigkeit ausscheidet, um sich unkenntlich zu machen?« –
– »Der Tintenfisch und seine Flüssigkeit sind ein Gemeinplatz!« –
– »Aber kennst du das Geräusch, das entsteht, wenn das Innere eines Krakens mit der Faust nach außen gerissen wird?« –
– »Ja, es lautet: KRÄCK!«

"When the horsemen of the apocalypse come we'll lie down on the dirt road and form a wagon wheel with our bodies." —
— "And if you are alone?" —
— "If I am alone, the horsemen of the apocalypse won't come."

Scarcely have I begun to look vainly for a sentence for something in my surroundings — already I feel painfully different from the surroundings.

"Do you know the difference between someone walking some distance from you at night with a flashlight and Saint Alexius under the stairs?" —
— "I know that sight! Someone has just died." —
— "Yes, you stepped on a mushroom, and the mushroom puffed dust on you as it exploded." —
— "So that's why the towels are dirty!"

Scarcely have I become one with my surroundings — already I begin to speak again and am different.

"Isn't it the squid that secretes a fluid to make itself unrecognizable?" —
— "The squid and its fluid are a cliché." —
— "But do you know the sound produced when a fist tears an octopus inside out?" —
— "Yes, it goes: CRAAK!"

Kaum fange ich zu reden an – schon höre ich mich
immer wieder: KRÄCK. KRÄCK.

»Kennst du das Geräusch, das entsteht, wenn die
Schlange über den Picknickkorb kriecht?« –
– »Ja, es lautet: KRÄCK. KRÄCK!« –
– »Gerade ist jemand gestorben!« –
– »Ja, das Geräusch kenne ich.«

Kaum fange ich zu reden an – schon scheiden alle
Gegenstände in meiner Umgebung eine Flüssigkeit
ab, die mich unkenntlich macht.

»Wußtest du schon, warum Erhängte die Beine an
sich ziehen?« –
– »Sie wollen ein Wagenrad bilden?« –
– »Nein, der Boden unter ihren Füßen ist voller
Schlangen!«

Kaum höre ich zu reden auf – schon unterscheide ich
im Vorhang und in den Handtüchern Löcher, die die
Heuschrecken hineingefressen haben.

»Wußtest du schon, daß jemand, der erfährt, daß
über den Jausenkorb, aus dem er gerade gegessen hat,
eine Schlange gekrochen ist, vor Grausen sofort sterben muß?« –
– »Ja, das steht in dem Buch über die Wilde Jagd.«

»Ist dir die Melodie, die der Hoteldiener dem Zimmermädchen auf dem Hügel vor dem Haus vorsummt, ein Begriff?« –

Scarcely have I begun to speak — already I hear myself over and over: CRAAK, CRAAK.

"Do you know the sound a snake makes when it crawls over a picnic basket?" —
— "Yes, it goes: CRAAAK, CRAAK." —
— "Someone has just died." —
— "Yes, I know that sound."

Scarcely have I begun to speak — already all objects in my surroundings secrete a fluid that makes me unrecognizable.

"Did you know why hanged men draw up their legs?" —
— "They want to form a wagon wheel?" —
— "No, the ground under their feet is crawling with snakes!"

Scarcely have I stopped speaking — already I distinguish holes in the curtain and towels which the grasshoppers have made.

"Did you know that someone who finds out that a snake has crawled over the picnic basket from which he has just been picnicking, that that someone straightaway dies of fright?" —
— "Yes, so it stands written in the book about the horse-men of the apocalypse."

"Are you familiar with the melody the bellboy is humming to the chambermaid on the hill in front of the house?" —

– »Ja, aber mir fehlt das Wort dafür!« –
– »Es ist das Lied vom Heiligen Alexius unter der Stiege.«

Kaum höre ich niemanden mehr sprechen – schon übersetze ich mir heimlich die Gegenstände, die ich wahrnehme, in Worte, und kaum habe ich mir die Gegenstände übersetzt – schon sind sie mir ein Begriff.

»Dieses Geräusch kenne ich! Der Hoteldiener summt eine Melodie von Henry Mancini!« –
– »Nein, der Pilz, der dich anstaubt, heißt Bovist!«

Kaum habe ich angefangen zu schauen – schon ist aus dem Vorhang ein Anblick geworden.

»Weißt du, warum der Hoteldiener dem Zimmermädchen auf dem Hügel vor dem Haus eine Melodie von Henry Mancini vorsummt?« –
– »Ja, weil das Zimmermädchen Angst hat, in der Nacht auf einem Feldweg zu gehen.« –
– »Ja, das Wort ›taghell‹ bedeutet, daß es noch Nacht ist.«

Kaum habe ich Worte für das, was ich wahrnehme – schon erscheinen mir die Worte für dies und für jenes als Witz.

»Kennst du den Unterschied zwischen –?« –
– »Ja, der Unterschied ist ein Witz!« –

— "Yes, but I don't know the word for it."
— "It is the song of Saint Alexius under the stairs."

Scarcely have I stopped hearing anyone speak — already I am secretly translating objects I perceive into words, and scarcely have I finished translating the objects — already I have a concept of them.

"I know that sound! The bellboy is humming a melody by Henry Mancini." —
— "No, the mushroom that puffed dust on you is called bovist!"

Scarcely have I begun to look — already the curtain becomes a sight.

"Do you know why the bellboy is humming a Henry Mancini melody to the chambermaid on the hill in front of the house?" —
— "Yes, because the chambermaid is afraid of walking on the dirt road at night." —
— "Yes, the phrase 'as bright as day' means it is still night."

Scarcely have I found words for what I perceive — already the words for this or that seem like a joke to me.

"Do you know the difference between — ?" —
— "Yes, the difference is a joke!"

– »Ja, nur was in Sätzen, die sich gleichen, unterge-
bracht werden kann, unterscheidet sich.«

Kaum habe ich keinen Satz mehr für das, was ich
wahrnehme – schon erscheint mir dies und jenes, was
ich wahrnehme, als das äußerste AUSLAND, und kaum
fange ich wieder zu reden an – schon erscheint mir
jeder Satz als ein Traum von dem, was ich wahrnehme.

»Gerade ist jemand gestorben!« –
– »Ja, aber im Ausland.« –
– »Gerade wird da etwas von INNEN nach AUSSEN
gestülpt!« –
– »Ja, aber im Ausland.« –
– »Gerade macht da etwas KRÄCK!« –
– »Ja, aber weil wir davon reden können, ist es ein
Traum.«

— "Yes, only what can be accommodated in sentences that resemble each other are different from each other."

Scarcely have I reached the point where I have not a single sentence for what I perceive — already this and that which I perceive appears to me like the most outlandish outlandishness, and I have scarcely begun to speak again — already each sentence seems like a dream of what I perceive.

"Someone has just died!" —
— "Yes, but in the outlands." —
— "Something is just being turned inside out!" —
— "Yes, but in the outlands." —
— "Something is just going CRAAK!" —
— "Yes, but because we can speak of it it is a dream."

Erschrecken

Beim Telefonieren, als ich im Nacken einen Luftzug
                                                    spüre,
steht plötzlich niemand hinter mir, und ich
                                            erschrecke;
im Bad, unter der Dusche, steht plötzlich niemand
                            hinter mir, und ich erschrecke:

— erschrecken:
über das auf den Steinboden fallende Geschirr, das
                                            aus Holz ist
über die Spielkarten, die alle in das Etui passen
über die Stufe, die dem Schild ACHTUNG STUFE folgt:

erschrecken über etwas, auf das man gefaßt ist, und
über etwas erschrecken, auf das man nicht gefaßt ist,
und über etwas erschrecken, auf das man nicht gefaßt
ist, weil man gefaßt war, über etwas *anderes* zu erschrecken, und über *nichts,* weil man gefaßt war, über
etwas zu erschrecken, erschrecken:

— erschrecken:
über den an der Scheibe herunterlaufenden Tropfen
                    erschrecken, der plötzlich stehenbleibt
über den Ball erschrecken, der vom Lastwagen *nicht*
                                            überfahren wird

Fright

While I am telephoning I feel a draft at my neck
and suddenly no one stands behind me, and I am frightened;
in the bathroom under the shower suddenly no one stands
behind me, and I am frightened:

— to be frightened:
by wooden plates falling on the stone floor
by playing cards that fit into the case
by the step that follows the sign STEP DOWN

to be frightened by something which one anticipates, and
to be frightened by something which one does not antic-
ipate because one anticipates being frightened by something *else*, and to be startled by *nothing* because one anticipated being frightened by *something*:

to be frightened:
by the raindrop running down the pane coming to a
sudden stop
by the ball that is *not* squashed by the truck

über die Türklinke, an der die Hand *nicht* abrutscht,
erschrecken
und über die zufallende Tür, die man noch vor dem
Einschnappen erreicht, erschrecken

– erschrecken über jede Zeitung, aus der keine
Beilage fällt
über jede Haarsträhne im Gesicht, die keine
Schnittwunde ist
über das Nichtausgleiten auf dem Eis erschrecken
über das Nichtdrücken der neuen Schuhe erschrecken
über das Nichtverschlossensein der fremden Tür
erschrecken:

– erschrecken: wenn ein Schlag einen anderen trifft
wenn man beim Aufspringen auf den
Zug nicht ausgleitet
wenn der Uniformierte, der auf einen
zulief, an einem vorbeiläuft:

– erschrecken darüber, daß ein Stein, den man in
einen Brunnen wirft, auf Grund trifft
darüber erschrecken, daß ein tollwütiger Hund durch
einen Zaun von einem getrennt ist
erschrecken darüber, daß ein eben zusammengerolltes
Papier sich von selber wieder entrollt
darüber erschrecken, daß die Hand die Fliege
gefangen hat
darüber, daß der nackte Fuß im Finstern auf keinen
Nagel tritt, erschrecken:

by the door handle that does *not* slip in one's hand
by the door that is falling shut but which you reach just
before it does fall shut

— to be frightened by every program without a com-
mercial
by every hair in the face which is not a cut
every time one does not slip on ice
every time a pair of new shoes does not pinch
every time an unfamiliar door is not locked:

to be frightened: when a blow hits someone else
when you do not fall when leaping onto
the moving train
when the uniform rushing towards you
rushes on past

— to be frightened by the fact that a stone that you have
tossed into a well hits the bottom of the well
to be frightened by the fact that a piece of paper you have
just rolled into a ball unfolds itself again of its own accord
to be frightened by the fact that the hand actually caught
the fly
to be frightened by the fact that one's naked foot does not
impale itself on a nail in the dark:

– Was für ein Schrecken!:
Der Mantelzipfel bleibt nicht in der Falltür hängen!
Die senkrecht gestellte Zigarette fällt nicht um!
Die Kastanie platzt nicht im Feuer!
Das Getreidefeld ist nicht niedergewalzt!
Die Augen des Pferdes sind frei von Fliegen!
Die Brücke ist nicht gesprengt!
Im Keller ist noch kein Rattengift gestreut!
Was für ein Schrecken!

– *Welcher* Schrecken?
Der Schrecken, der *nicht* eintritt, und der Schrecken,
der *noch* nicht eingetreten ist, und der Schrecken, der
eingetreten *ist* und wieder eintreten *wird,* und der
Schrecken, der *hier* nicht eintreten, und der Schrecken,
der *jetzt* nicht eintreten kann, und der Schrecken, für
dessen Eintritt gesorgt ist, und der Schrecken, der nur
gedacht werden kann, und der Schrecken, der *nicht*
gedacht werden kann, und der Schrecken darüber,
daß ein Schrecken nicht gedacht werden kann, und
der Schrecken über den Schrecken, der nicht mehr
schrecken kann:

– der Schrecken über jedes Grundstück, auf dem noch
                keine Selbstschüsse aufgestellt sind:

– »Dieser Randstein ist noch nicht umgefahren!«
»Dieses Plakat ist noch nicht abgefetzt!«
»Diese Juwelierscheibe ist noch nicht zertrümmert!«
»Dieses Auto ist noch nicht umgeworfen!«
»Dieser Pflasterstein ist noch nicht ausgegraben!«

— Oh, what a fright!:
The coattail is not caught in the trap door!
The cigar standing on its end does not fall over!
The chestnut does not explode in the fireplace!
The cornfield is not trampled flat!
The horse's eyes are free of flies!
The bridge is not blown up!
No rat poison has been set in the cellar!
Oh, what a fright!

— *Which* fright?
The fright which does *not* set in, and the fright which has not *yet* set in, and the fright which *has* set in and *will* set in again, and the fright which cannot set in *here* and the fright which cannot set in *now*, and the fright whose appearance is assured and the fright which can only be *imagined* and the fright which can *not* be imagined, and the fright over the fact *that* a fright cannot be imagined and the fright over the fright that can no longer frighten:

— the fright over every piece of land not studded with self-detonating explosives:

— "This curbstone has not been crushed yet!"
"This poster has not been torn off yet!"
"This jeweler's window has not been smashed in yet!"
"This car has not been turned over yet!"
"This paving stone has not been dug out yet!"

»Dieser Grenzstreifen ist noch nicht vermint!«
»Über diesen Kopf ist noch kein Nylonstrumpf
                                    gezogen!«
»Diese Telefonzelle ist noch nicht ausgebrannt!«
»Bei diesem Knall fliegt niemand durch die Luft!«
»Bei diesem Pfiff erscheint kein Polizeiauto!«
»Dieser Briefmarkenautomat gibt noch Briefmarken
                                    heraus!«
»Von diesem Untergetauchten sieht man noch
                                    Luftblasen!«
Was für ein Schrecken!
Was für ein Schrecken! –

– Erschrecken:
über alles Genießbare, an dem sich noch kein
                                    Preiszettel befindet
über jede Bank, die noch nicht ausgeraubt ist
über jedes Foto, auf dem noch keine gestrichelte Linie
                                    eingezeichnet ist
über jeden Laden, der noch nicht wegen Todesfall
                                    geschlossen ist
über jede Mücke auf dem Arm, die nicht zusticht
über jeden unterirdischen Gang, der noch nicht
                                    eingestürzt ist
über jeden Plünderer, der mit dem Teppich bis zum
                                    Lastwagen kommt,
                                    erschrecken:

– erschrecken über jeden *verfrühten, verspäteten*
                                    Schrecken:

"This border has not been mined yet!"
"This head has no nylon stocking over it yet!"
"This telephone booth hasn't been burnt yet!"
"At this explosion no one flies through the air!"
"At this whistle no police car appears!"
"This stamp machine still has stamps in it!"
"There are still air bubbles coming up from the one who
has just dived!"
What a fright!
What a fright! —

— to be frightened:
by everything enjoyable that doesn't have a price tag on
it yet
by every bank that hasn't been robbed yet
by every photo that hasn't been tampered with yet
by every store which isn't closed because of a death in the
family
by every mosquito on your arm that doesn't bite
by every underground passage that hasn't collapsed yet
by every thief who makes it out the front door:

— to be frightened by every *premature* and *belated* fright:

– »Wie furchtbar – dieser Pilz bewirkt keine
                              Krämpfe!«
»Wie entsetzlich – dieses Wort verletzt nicht!«
»Wie grauenhaft – dieser Ballon platzt nicht!«
»Wie schrecklich – dieses Grün ist nicht giftig!« –

– Der Verdurstende sieht, daß die Flasche noch nicht
                              leer ist;
Der Verirrte geht noch immer auf festem Boden;
Der Angegriffene sieht, daß der Angreifer die Faust
                      noch nicht geschlossen hat –
– wie sie erschrecken!
– wie sie erschrecken!

– erschrecken:
über jede leere Falle
über jedes leere Stadion
über jedes leere Unterholz –

– über jeden Ort, der sich auch in Wirklichkeit dort
befindet, wo ihn die Landkarte eingezeichnet hat –
erschrecken
erschrecken
erschrecken:

»der« – oh nein!
»die« – oh nein!
»das« – oh nein!

– erschrecken über *erschrecken*
erschrecken über *nicht* erschrecken

— "How awful — this mushroom produces no cramps!"
"How horrible — this word does not injure!"
"How terrible — this balloon does not explode!"
"How ghastly — this green is not poisonous!"

— The man who is dying of thirst sees that the bottle
isn't empty yet;
The man who is lost is still walking on firm ground;
The man who has been attacked sees that his attacker
hasn't closed his fist yet —
— how frightened they are!
— how frightened they are!

— to be frightened:
by every empty trap
by every empty stadium
by every empty doorway —

— by every place which really is where the map says it is —
to be frightened
to be frightened
to be frightened

"he" — oh no!
"she" — oh no!
"it" — oh no!

— to be frightened by *being frightened*
to be frightened by *not* being frightened

erschrecken über *sich freuen*
sich freuen über *erschrecken:*

– »Diese Lottokugel fällt ins Glas!«
»Dieses Loch im Eis hat nichts zu bedeuten!«
»In diesem Maisfeld hält sich niemand versteckt!«
»Diese Wüste ist eine Fata Morgana!«

to be frightened by *being happy*
to be happy about *being frightened*:

"This hole in the ice doesn't mean anything!"
"No one is hiding in this cornfield!"
"This desert is a Fata Morgana!"

Abbrechen mittem im Satz

Der letzte Satz des Märchenerzählers lautet gewöhnlich:

»Plötzlich, mitten im Bild, hörte der Pferdemaler zu malen auf und erwürgte den Herrenreiter.«

Plötzlich, mitten im letzten Satz –

Breaking Off in Mid-Sentence

The fairy-tale's last sentence usually goes:

"Suddenly, in the middle of the picture, the horse painter stopped painting and strangled the gentleman-jockey."

Suddenly, in the middle of the last sentence —

"What I ask of literature is something new, something that changes me if only slightly, something that makes me aware of an as yet unthought-of, an as yet unconscious possibility of reality, of a new possibility of seeing, of speaking, of thinking, of existing. Ever since I discovered that I was able to change myself through literature, that literature had made me into someone else, I continue to expect of literature always a new possibility for changing myself, because I don't regard myself as unchangeable. And because I recognized that I could change myself through literature, that it was because of literature that I could live with a higher degree of awareness, I also became convinced that I might be able to change others with my literature."

"The progress of literature seems to me to consist of the gradual removal of unnecessary fictions. More and more vehicles fall by the wayside, the story becomes superfluous, invention becomes super-fluous, what matters more is the communication of experiences, linguistic and non-linguistic ones, and for that it is no longer necessary to invent stories."

"I never thought I would write plays. Theater as it exists was for me a relic from the past. Brecht and Beckett didn't have anything to do with me either. The stories on stage had nothing to do with me; instead of being simple they were invariably simplifications. The possibilities of reality were limited through the impossibilities of the stage, theater deceived about reality . . . reality was feigned where there was fiction."

—Peter Handke, from "I Am an Inhabitant of the Ivory Tower"

Postscript: A Note on Methods

"Whether a more precise awareness of the spectators and auditors produces an impetus to change the conditions in the Marxist sense (which would also be mine) of that I have my doubts, although I wish it were the case; that is, I become increasingly more doubtful the more I wish for it: the theater in the theater probably only creates new possibilities for thinking."

Peter Handke

One can speculate that Peter Handke initially lacked any but avant-garde resources; that he shared with the fertile avant-garde ambience* where he began to produce its by-now traditional animadversion to the dominant literary tradition of the time. Which meant that this aversion, this ennui with the once used, this compulsion to find ever new personally and historically appropriate ways of expression would eventually result, as it indeed has in Handke's case, in a turning against these avant-garde origins and traditions too, without — and this should perhaps be self-evident — a reversion to the dominant

---

* As distinct from West German literature, postwar Austrian literature can be characterized chiefly by that portmanteau label "avant-garde." There are even two opposing "avant-garde" directions, one located in Vienna, the other in Graz. Most of the important writers from both camps are quite unknown in this country. They include: H. C. Artmann, Oswald Wiener, Konrad Bayer, Thomas Bernhard, Gerhard Rühm, Friedrich Achleitner, to mention only the best known of them. Ingeborg Bachmann, too, was Austrian.

tradition against which he had initially revolted. That he would remain faithful only to the original basis of this revolt, the impetus for constant transformation, which is a response to contemporary life itself: so that his singular progress — singular in Western literature in the last decade — may be regarded as a gradual synthesis of a large variety of avant-garde techniques into a confident, authoritative, sovereign narrative and dramatic style of his own which now bears few if any of the earmarks of avant-gardism.

At one time fatalistically resigned to *methods,* and making the best of an overt use of them (i.e. that the artificiality of literary methods has to be evident in the work, since methods become useless when the awareness of their essential artificiality is lost, when they come to seem "natural") to a careless reader Handke's latest work may even bear some resemblance to the truly traditional. Yet these newest works would be unthinkable without what has come before, and most of what came first already superseded its avant-garde origins in that it can stand on its own apart from an avant-garde context. German critics, only so recently troubled by what they regarded as Handke's ebullient avant-gardism, whose success they were unable to explain, now grumble about his alleged classicism.

Though not necessarily published in chronological order in this country, much of Handke's work is now in English, and the important novel *Der Hausierer* (1967) may eventually become available too. In all of this work up until but not including *Short Letter, Long Goodbye* (1972) we notice that Handke has devised particular methods and techniques to involve the audience in his plays, novel and poems, to affect the audience's consciousness, to create experiences above and beyond those heretofore associated with the attendance of a theatrical event or the reading of a text. Having germinated in an avant-garde environment, these methods and techniques here are suddenly put to a consistent, esthetically logical use for the expression and creation of major experiences. It is important to describe some of these methods and principles, for they were scarcely devised for their own sake or out of idle experimentation. Their invention and their use (aside from personal necessity) is the consequence of the status of the theatrical and written media in the age of television, film and electronically amplified music.

These methods have to do with what is required to refashion the theater and texts, so that what they can do (and the purely visual and aural media cannot) has an opportunity to penetrate, affect and possibly alter the consciousness, and thus also the lives, of their audience. Yet the comparison, say between theater and film, is not as easy as standing them side by side. Nothing could be more apparent than that each, as a medium, does certain things the other cannot do: you merely have to attend the performance of a filmed play. What counts, I think, is something like this: compared to film, television and contemporary music, the theater and texts appear to offer quantitatively fewer stimuli, are closer to being second-hand experiences — or at least appear to be, which is all that matters for my purposes here (it is not merely a question of talent) and consequently make the wrong kinds of demands on their audience's concentration and imagination; are more fictional, too derived, too indirect. For the sake of argument I would offer this as a temporarily undifferentiated absolute on the simple level of sensory stimulation provided and perceived. As bereft of deep and affecting content as television and film may be, they nonetheless provide a gross habituating output of sheer stimulation (estheticism at its quantitatively highest but qualitatively lowest), so that if the theater and the written text want to affect the audience they have little choice but to present their quality, their special content, with something that intrinsically approximates the potency of the visual and aural media.

This does not mean a superficial copying or adaptation of the techniques of the visual and aural media into a written or theatrical context (the entire multi-media syndrome in any event is more of a symptom than a solution to the problem), but to find intrinsic methods by which to extend the effect of the theater and the written text; and this necessary extension is what perhaps constitutes the inexorable influence of the visual and aural media on writing and theater in our time. It is to this challenge that Handke has had no choice but to address himself.

Public Insult*, Handke's first major play, written when he was 22, and already a synthesis of numerous avant-garde methods and a major attempt to find a more direct way of communicating with the audience, constitutes a complete inversion of traditional theatrical procedure. Instead of sitting back and watching a play, the audience

---

* As for many things, I am indebted to Herbert Berghof, who directed the first professional performance of *Publikumsbeschimpfung* in this country, also for the adequate title of that play in English: *Public Insult*.

itself and its experience in the theater become the topic of the play. For roughly one hour the audience is addressed. The four speakers who address it portray no parts, act merely as mouthpieces. The audience sits in the crossfire of their words. The text is allocated to the speakers as the director sees fit. The speakers can speak singly, in pairs, in threes or in chorus. What is required for the play is as much a director as a musical conductor and choreographer, because pacing and the rhythms of delivery and the alternating group picture are of ultimate importance. It is clear that we are dealing here with the integration of musical and literary forms, not with a simple mixture.

The audience's attention is not allowed to digress for a second; not simply because it is being addressed but because what it is being told immediately applies to its situation as an audience in the theater. Because everything applies and as it applies is also proved to the audience, the audience begins to resist this insistent methodical onslaught; it does not walk out because it keeps reassuring itself that, after all, this is only theater, which is true enough: but that is the psychological element — the compulsion to make believe that this is all make believe, which is the opposite of the usual attempt to suspend disbelief — that the play turns to its advantage.

Aside from statements whose truth is obvious, one method that the play employs to break down the audience's resistance is logic: both serious and scholastically and legally perverse and devious. Another unsettling method is the constant alternation between seriousness and admission of playfulness (but a real play "like the sixty minutes of a football game") which amounts to an incessant now you see it now you don't. Since all these methods work in unison, are reinforced by the rhythms with which the text is delivered, they cannot help but produce an exceptional state of heightened consciousness and self-awareness. By taking the attendance of a theatrical event utterly seriously the audience's existence, if only that one hour of existence in the theater, is thoroughly theatricalized; and the attendance of this play now becomes an existential event. By extension, it makes the audience question not only its theatrical mode of behavior and thinking, but potentially all other forms of behavior and thinking.

Public Insult is designed to alter and make more precise the audience's consciousness. And what is remarkable is that this is done by making useful for the play's purposes every convention of the traditional theater, including the confining space of the spectator room itself (the play works best in a relatively small crowded space). Logic and literary convention remain in control throughout. The means are inherent in the medium. The invective at the end of the play, which gave it its name and initial fame (or notoriety), are a mischievous test of whether the audience understands the bravura game that has been played with theatricality and reality, the two levels that have alternated throughout. The invective covers all bases, consists of rhythmically and acoustically arranged patterns of insults which, as a matter of fact, cancel each other out. That is a very Austrian joke.

Self-Accusation, written at about the same time as *Public Insult* but only half as long, is in some respects even sparser. It has only two speakers, one male one female. The text they speak, also directed at the audience, con-

sists almost entirely of brief declarative sentences:
Self-Accusation begins:

"I came into the world

I became. I was begotten. I originated. I grew. I was born. I was entered in the birth register. I grew older."

And ends:

"I am not what I was. I was not what I should have been. I did not become what I should have become. I did not keep what I should have kept.

I went to the theater. I heard this piece. I spoke this piece. I wrote this piece."

Between these two points *Self-Accusation* recounts the process of growing up and becoming guilty in a totally original manner. Being in a confessional mode it of course lacks the abrasive quality and intent of *Public Insult*: the confessional mode elicits the audience's sympathy, the patterned method counteracts it. Like *Public Insult* it does entirely without stage props, directing the audience's attention that much more forcefully toward the words.

These two manifestly verbal plays were followed by *My Foot My Tutor*, a play without words but with a prominent set and music and sounds instead. Within an ironically idyllic, patently stagey bucolic setting a farmer and his servant (the "tutor" and his "foot") act out a not totally intelligible game of domination and slowly growing insurgency. The striking set without words is like the obverse of the previous plays with their striking language on a bare stage. The deprivation of one sense increases the sensitivity of another. Within this theatrical setting the apparently meaningful but nonetheless incomprehensible interaction of these two actors produces a form of puzzlement which allows us to become aware of something which we would not become aware of if each action were properly motivated by verbal justification. We become aware of the structure of the interaction, of patterns of behavior of each of the two actors who fail to proclaim any of the justifications, based on the reality principle, to which we are accustomed; consequently we may come to question the reality principle that does govern their actions. The play can be described as semi-ritualized, just as it is semi-realistic in some respects: the set consists of a curious combination of partially "real" and partially "artificial" props. The overall structure of the piece, which is accentuated by the repeat chords from Country Joe & The Fish's *Colors for Susan*, creates a general mood similar to a suspension of time, a stasis which is useful esthetically as well as scientifically.

In *Kaspar* (1968) Handke combines and extends the methods of the three previous plays. In *Public Insult* the audience was addressed directly; in the first act of *Kaspar*, by undergoing the speech torture to which Kaspar is subjected together with him, it is addressed indirectly. Kaspar acts out the pain the audience, which empathizes with him, might feel if it were addressed directly. As Kaspar is educated he learns to associate words with what he sees, and we come to experience the actual fusion of the visual and verbal elements. Its two great monologues extend the confessional mode of *Self-Accusation*. Handke's achievement in *Kaspar* is to have reduced the process of the education of an individual to purely linguistic terms, into language education — from simple grammar to its ultimate result: the frantic mouthing of liberal platitudes — without resorting to allegory, to any kind of fiction at all. For what we watch and undergo is not a reenactment of the Kaspar Hauser story, useful as that may be to some in sorting out their experience of the play, but the presentation of an educational process entirely in terms of theatrical actions which have to be experienced before they can be understood. *Kaspar* exists first of all on a pre-conceptual, purely experiential level. It is, as it were, a totally concrete metaphor.

The short but difficult *Quodlibet* (1970) is chiefly notable for its attempt to adapt the principle of auditory hallucination to the stage. The personages of the "world stage" — presidents, bishops, CIA men, etc. — parade around mouthing increasingly more ambiguous words and sentences with scatological, sexual and criminal connotations: a growing series of double, triple and quadruple entendres. The demands made on the audience are quite extraordinary, and it is questionable whether the rewards are commensurate with these demands. Whether in fact, even if the audience listens as carefully as possible — and of course the more carefully it listens, the more over- and undertones it begins to hear, depending on how sophisticated it is, a sophistication which on the one hand also indicts it, for the simple may not hear any connotations at all — it will realize that the connotations that are suggested by the words spoken on stage, are primarily the creation of its own ambiguous state of mind.

Like *Kaspar* and all of Handke's plays until then, *The Ride Across Lake Constance* is non-imitative and refers to no reality outside itself to make itself intelligible. Handke breaks the world and the stage completely apart so as to make the theatrical experience a unique experience in the theater and, therefore, also a unique part of one's life in the world. His plays are events in themselves. His apparent non-realism thinks the idea of realism to the end, for what he seeks to create is something completely real, not an illusion of a reality we already know.

The Ride Across Lake Constance calls for eight actors, three men and four women who are to be listed in the program as playing themselves, and one other woman. Actors onstage who don't have to portray a character cannot be anything but actors. People who appear onstage in a play are automatically actors. So the only identity these characters have is that of actors. The objects cannot be anything but props, the scenery is scenery only.

Nor does this play have a plot one could recount to summarize the play in terms of its skeleton. Since the play does not *describe* anything outside the theater, one of course cannot refer to the world outside the theater to describe the play. The two are not comparable in normal realistic fashion.

As we experience the play onstage or stage it in our imagination, our apprehension, our puzzlement, and our feeling of estrangement increases. We are disconcerted. We don't know what to make of what we are experiencing. If *My Foot My Tutor* was a relatively straightforward demonstration of behavioral patterns, *Ride Across Lake*

Constance, as Richard Gilman has pointed out, is a fully orchestrated play.*

What we experience are eight actors who are simply *there*, onstage. Their situation is unquestionably existential as well as theatrical — the two being inextricably linked in any case. They exist, we do not know who they are; all we know is that they are actors. They are playing, all they do is play. They lack essence. Everything is artificial. What they play on stage makes an improvisational impression. They discover who they are onstage in terms of each other, give each other identities, play identities, are captured by their identities — their identities become their roles or vice versa; are held together by the relationships they establish with each other — which at first are only a playing, but into which they get locked. They establish rules for each other, enslave each other with behavioral and linguistic rules. Sometimes they just play and their existence onstage becomes delightfully easy; everything seems to fit. Yet all their elaborate charades are devoid of the customary psychological and realistic motivation; they take place in a purely theatrical setting, and so do not become comprehensible to us within a framework of ordinary day-to-day experience, or what we think that is. There are no reference points for us, the audience; just as little as there are for the actors onstage. They are exceedingly vulnerable; as a matter of fact, one can probably generalize and say that they get locked into their roles more out of fear than anything else. Everything they play, even their very playfulness, is always unexpected, not to

* "Peter Handke" by Richard Gilman, *American Review* 17, 1973.

be anticipated. Everything is slightly off-center, but only slightly; there appears to be a logic to their talk and their behavior, but it isn't quite our logic. So we begin to feel a peculiar tension, a double effect produced by the disparity between what we are experiencing and what we are familiar with. What we are experiencing seems eerily familiar, and if we try to think of something that might induce a similar state of apprehension — ominousness, ludicrousness, perverse logic and yet hypnotizing familiarity — only a dream comes to mind. ("Are you dreaming or are you speaking?" is the play's epigraph.) The repeated, yet unfathomable, cutting against the grain of normal expectation gradually produces such a state of uncertainty and heightened awareness that we no longer know whether we are participating in a dream or something real; indeed, there is no question but that the dream *is* real.

Handke, of course, is not duplicating a dream onstage. We are forced to participate in an event that has the dissociative effect of a dream. Through an intense experience of estrangement we may possibly become aware of the strangeness, the artificiality of the world outside the theater. To anyone who has worked intensively on *Ride Across Lake Constance* most conversations in the real world will sound ludicrous for a long time. What the play makes us aware of is our unawareness of that artificial, ludicrous dimension in our lives, which no longer seem that natural, that unchangeable; of the fragility of identities, the evanescence of feelings; of the whole world of unreality, of unawareness that surrounds our lives. That aspect of existence is, of course, made much more effectively apparent through a theatrical method that makes us experience it rather than one that describes or conceptualizes it for us.

I will reserve comment on Handke's latest play *They Are Dying Out* (1973) because the methods employed there are not particularly pertinent to a reading of *Innerworld*. However, I would like to make the briefest mention of the methods of two of the novels, if only to suggest the great variety of Handke's methodological repertoire. *Der Hausierer* forces the reader to supply what the usual novel ordinarily depends on: description and the whole connective tissue of plot. In fact, it forces the reader to invent the novel for himself. *The Goalie's Anxiety at the Penalty Kick* (1970) manages to induce in the careful reader through purely syntactic means a similar state of mind as that of the protagonist.

Though written over a four year period, most of the poems from *Innerworld* were composed in 1967 and 1968. After the description of some of Handke's techniques and methods, these poems will be perhaps somewhat less unusual than they might otherwise. I would think it will be immediately apparent what poetic devices these poems dispense with and what has replaced them: the chief principle underlying nearly all these poems is the *series*. The series becomes the medium. It creates a world — an artificial world — of its own with its own time within which the poet creates his effects, be it by means of timing, variation, contrast, contraposition, accumulation, crescendo and de-crescendo, etc. At its simplest we find the series in a poem such as "The Three Readings of the Law." The first stanza gives the statement; the second the qualifications; and the third the bitterly ironic resolution. The most complex example is probably "Distinctions" with its interjecting voices; almost like a micro-play. As a matter of fact, it is remarkable how effective these poems are when read aloud to an audience. There is the use of shock-effect, at its most overt in "Comparisons for What's Incomparable," the creation of pure haiku-like stasis as in "Singular and Plural." As long as one does not demand of these poems that they produce the effects one might expect poetry to have, the experiences which they create for the reader should be able to affect him or her. But once they have been experienced, that experience ideally continues to have a lasting effect with which everyone may do as he pleases.

I want to thank Karen Crossen Ready for a very careful reading of the translation and for many useful suggestions.

MICHAEL ROLOFF

1974

Biographical Note

Peter Handke was born in 1942 in Griffen, Austria, into, as he has said, "a worker's family." However, if we are to trust the description of the life of this family (as it comes to us in *Sorrow Beyond Pity*, Handke's only major autobiographical work to date*) it was a "worker's" only in the sense of how it made its living, not in the sense it had of itself. For, as Handke notes with chagrin, this family was devoid of proletarian class consciousness.

Handke's secondary education comprised several years at a Catholic seminary which prepared its charges for the priesthood, and two years at a more standard educational institution, a *Humanistisches Gymnasium*. After graduating from the latter in 1959, he studied law at the University of Graz. He chose the study of law, he has said, to allow himself as much time as possible to write (four years of legal studies could be crammed into the six months prior to final exams) and because a law degree can be a useful entree into the Austrian diplomatic service, a career Handke had considered because he felt it might provide him with more time than any other in which to write. Handke has stated that he began to write at age twelve. It appears that his life has been governed by this ineluctable ambition ever since.

---

* *Sorrow Beyond Pity* seeks to come to terms with his mother's suicide, but of course does so unsuccessfully from his point of view.

Bibliography

PETER HANDKE'S WORK IN ORDER OF THE DATES OF COMPOSITION:

1963-64 *Die Hornissen (The Hornets)*

1964-1965 *Publikumsbeschimpfung, Weissagung, Selbstbezichtigung, Hilfe-Rufe (Public Insult, Prophecy, Self-Accusation, Distress Calls)*

1963-66 *Begrüssung des Aufsichtsrats (Welcoming the Board of Directors)*

1965-66 *Der Hausierer (The Peddler)*

1967 *Kaspar*

1968 *Das Mündel will Vormund sein (My Foot My Tutor)*

1965-1968 *Die Innenwelt der Aussenwelt der Innenwelt (The Innerworld of the Outerworld of the Innerworld)*

1969 *Die Angst des Tormann's beim Elfmeter (The Goalie's Anxiety at the Penalty Kick); Quodlibet*

1968-70 *Hörspiele (Radio Plays)*

1970 *Chronik der laufenden Ereignisse (Chronicle of Current Events); Der Ritt über den Bodensee (The Ride Across Lake Constance)*

1971 *Der Kurze Brief zum langen Abschied (Short Letter, Long Farewell)*

1972 *Wunschloses Unglück (Sorrow Beyond Pity)*

1973 *Die Unvernünftigen sterben aus (They Are Dying Out)*

PETER HANDKE'S WORK IN ENGLISH:

Kaspar and Other Plays (including *Public Insult* and *Self-Accusation*), Farrar, Straus & Giroux, 1969

Distress Calls and *My Foot My Tutor*, in TDR 49, 1970.

The Ride Across Lake Constance, in *Contemporary German Drama*, edited by Michael Roloff, Avon Books, 1972

The Goalie's Anxiety at the Penalty Kick, Farrar, Straus & Giroux, 1972.

Kaspar (stage version), London: Eyre, Methuen, 1972.

Sorrow Beyond Pity, American Review #20, 1974.

Short Letter, Long Farewell, Farrar, Straus & Giroux, 1974.

To be published by Farrar, Straus & Giroux: *They Are Dying Out* and *Der Hausierer* (The Peddler).